STORYNOMICS

Also by Robert McKee

Film Works

*Story: Substance, Structure, Style,
and the Principles of Screenwriting*

*Dialogue: The Art of Verbal Action for
the Page, Stage, and Screen*

STORYNOMICS

Story-Driven Marketing in the
Post-Advertising World

by
R O B E R T M c K E E

and

T H O M A S G E R A C E

TWELVE

NEW YORK · BOSTON

Twelve

Hachette Book Group

1290 Avenue of the Americas, New York, NY 10104

twelvebooks.com

twitter.com/twelvebooks

First Hardcover Edition: March 2018

Twelve is an imprint of Grand Central Publishing. The Twelve name and logo are trademarks of Hachette Book Group, Inc.

The publisher is not responsible for websites (or their content) that are not owned by the publisher.

The Hachette Speakers Bureau provides a wide range of authors for speaking events. To find out more, go to www.hachettespeakersbureau.com or call (866) 376-6591.

Library of Congress Cataloging-in-Publication Data

Names: McKee, Robert, 1941- author. | Gerace, Thomas, author.
Title: Storynomics : story-driven marketing in the post-advertising world / Robert McKee and Thomas Gerace.
Description: New York : Twelve, [2018]
Identifiers: LCCN 2017042100| ISBN 9781538727935 (hardcover) | ISBN 9781549167454 (audio download) | ISBN 9781455541973 (ebook)
Subjects: LCSH: Marketing. | Storytelling.
Classification: LCC HF5415 .M26125 2018 | DDC 658.8—dc23
LC record available at https://lccn.loc.gov/2017042100

ISBNs: 978-1-5387-2793-5 (hardcover), 978-1-4555-4197-3 (ebook), 978-1-5491-6745-4 (audiobook, downloadable)

Printed in the United States of America

LSC-C

10 9 8 7 6 5 4 3 2 1

CONTENTS

CONTENTS

To Mia,
Her love gives all things meaning.
—Robert McKee

To my parents, Ann Jones Gerace and Samuel Philip
Gerace, who taught me to love a good story.
—Tom Gerace

ACKNOWLEDGMENTS

We offer special thanks to Mia Kim for her inspired and tireless leadership of the entire Storynomics enterprise. We would still be outlining if Mia had not kept us on task.

We are grateful to Linda Boff of GE, Raja Rajamannar of Mastercard, Caleb Barlow of IBM, Jeanniey Mullen of Mercer, Natalie Malaszenko of Overstock, David Beebe of Marriott, and Patrick Davis of Davis Brand Capital who graciously shared their time and wisdom with us.

We owe thanks too to Tricia Travaline, Genevieve Colton, Adam Vavrek, Ruben Sanchez, and Dara Cohen who have done heavy lifting to make the Storynomics enterprise a success. We are grateful to Marcia Friedman and Tom Hardej, who edited our early copy and helped ensure consistency of voice, and to Carl Rosendorf, Ann Gerace, Darryl Gehly, Dan Baptiste, Rob Murray, Caleb Gonsalves, Lauren Meyer, Michael Gowen, Kent Lawson, Bob Dekoch, Jim Rossmeissi, and others at Skyword, Boldt, and beyond, who read early drafts of the book and provided invaluable feedback along the way. And we thank Jim Manzi, for his unwavering support and belief in the power of story to drive change.

I will hazard a prediction. When you are 80 years old and in a quiet moment of reflection, narrating for only yourself the most personal version of your life's story, the telling that will be most compact and meaningful will be the series of choices you have made. In the end, we are our choices.

—Jeff Bezos, 2010 Princeton
Commencement Address

STORYNOMICS

INTRODUCTION

THE MARKETING CRISIS

Look around. It's happening. In ever-escalating millions, consumers are cutting the barbed wire of ad-imprisoned media and disappearing into a forest of paid subscriptions and ad blockers. No use searching for these people. They're gone and they're never coming back.

Now look ahead. Before long, all public and private communication—entertainment, news, music, sports, social media, online searches—will be ad-free, leaving sides of buses as the publicity medium of last resort.

Millennials, that vital under-forty market, are not only banishing advertising from their lives but sneering at the institution itself, denouncing its bragging and promising as deceitful, manipulative, the next thing to micro-aggression. In fact, a recent study revealed that over the past five years, television viewing by people under forty dropped 30 percent, while ad-free over-the-top services like Netflix skyrocketed.[1]

This massive consumer exit and the resulting drop in ad revenue has tossed umpteen media firms—Tribune Media, 21st Century Media, SBC Media, Relativity Media, Cumulus Media, Next Media, Citadel Broadcasting, the *Sun-Times*, Borders,

Blockbuster, *Reader's Digest*, and dozens more multibillion-dollar corporations—into the Dumpsters of bankruptcy.[2]

In 2015, 76 percent of marketers surveyed by Adobe claimed that marketing had changed more in the last two years than it had in all the decades since the birth of television. Many chief marketing officers swear they will never again trust advertising to deliver customers. Some CMOs condemn ad agencies for wasting time and money trying to be Super Bowl–creative instead of market-effective. Others blame the noise from free online ads that drowns out their paid ads. Still others complain that falling return on investment (ROI) and rising costs make advertising just too damn expensive. Of course, if advertising suddenly redelivered the mass consumers of decades past, all would be forgiven.

The more the push strategies of bragging and promising lose traction, the more marketers turn to the pull tactics of effective storytelling. To support their efforts, the *Harvard Business Review* has published dozens of articles on the persuasive power of story for both leadership and branding, a myriad of TED talks have championed the neuroscience behind storified messaging, and how-to writers have poured out dozens upon dozens of story-in-business manuals that could fill a wall at Barnes & Noble.

But despite published enthusiasm, boardroom misgivings about the nature and use of story run as wide and deep as ever. Now and then, an inspired campaign uses story to effect (for instance, the "What's the Matter with Owen?" campaign by GE, "Misunderstood" by Apple, or "Click, Baby, Click!" by Adobe),[3] but overall, corporate storytelling continues to sputter and stumble in confusion, more a trend than a tool. This is true not only for the marketing arms of most companies, but also for the PR and ad agencies that service them. The dream of story-driven commerce is still a dream. With *Storynomics*, we intend to turn this dream into reality.

Part 1, "The Marketing Revolution," investigates the problem. Once the causes of a crisis are exposed, its cure becomes self-evident. Chapter 1, "Advertising, A Story of Addiction," asks, "What went wrong?" and traces the rise and fall of advertising from Ben Franklin to today. Chapter 2, "Marketing, A Story of Deception," traces the problem back beyond advertising to the taproot of marketing logic.

Part 2, "Story Creation," explores the solution. The next four chapters examine the core elements of story, how they fit the mind, how they move consumer action, and how to design them for effect. Chapter 3, "The Evolution of Story," begins with the first human thought and follows the mind's evolution into storied consciousness. Chapter 4, "The Definition of Story," lays out the components of the universal, timeless form that underlies all storytelling in all cultures. Chapter 5, "The Full Story," delves deeper into the elements of story to help the reader develop her craft. Chapter 6, "The Purpose-Told Story," takes the reader through the step-by-step process for designing the ideal marketing story.

Part 3, "Putting Story to Work," turns solution into action. To transform the way your organization connects to its customers, you must harness your marketing, branding, advertising, and sales to the pulling power of story. The following chapters show you how to storify all four voices. Chapter 7, "Story and the CMO," casts the marketer as the master storyteller who envisions a campaign and then guides creatives as they transform the concept into storified action. Chapter 8, "Storified Branding," demonstrates the use of story to overcome the public's antipathy to corporations and win brand affinity. Chapter 9, "Storified Advertising," argues that ads work best when the interruption tells a story that hooks, holds, and entertains. Chapter 10, "Storified Demand and Lead Generation," looks at how thinking and planning in story form guides marketing's grand strategy and takes your corporation to long-term success. Chapter 11, "Building Audience," explains how brands can integrate into the digital ecosystem to earn and expand audience, allowing the stories they tell to reach the masses. Chapter 12, "Storified Sales," lays out the full range of face-to-face storytelling options from point of sale to the viral cascade known as word of mouth. Chapter 13, "-Nomics," demonstrates how marketers can directly measure the value of their storytelling and compare its efficacy with that of traditional advertising.

The conclusion, "Tomorrow," looks forward, forecasting the impact of new and upcoming technological change on the use of storytelling in marketing. We examine how the impact of story will continue to grow, and our ability to create immersive experiences will take a leap forward, while essential story form remains the same.

Justin Smith, CEO of Bloomberg Media Group, said, "All business is bifurcated into two distinct worlds: the struggling traditional segment that longs for a simpler, more profitable past that will never return; and the vibrant, entrepreneurial segment that is reinventing commerce before our eyes."

This book was written for you reinventors. We coined the infinitive *to storify* to name the transformation of data into story form, the adjective *storified* to describe data that has undergone that change, and the noun *Storynomics* to title the story-centric business practices that drive fiscal results.

The difference between data and story is this: Data lists what happened; story expresses how and why it happened. Data compiles facts by quantity and frequency; story reveals the causalities behind and beneath those facts. Story eliminates irrelevancies, concentrates on dynamic change, and then reshapes factual subject matter into a structure that links events into chains of cause and effect, played out over time.

Storynomics taps this enormous potential in the business world. Those marketers who master storytelling techniques will plant and harvest a timeless bounty as they invent the future.

PART I

THE MARKETING REVOLUTION

1

ADVERTISING, A STORY OF ADDICTION

It started innocently enough. In the 1700s, weekly newspapers detailing local life and politics in the American colonies first sprouted everywhere, but then shriveled and died for two reasons. One, printing required a license from the Crown that specifically prohibited satire of the king's representatives. A cartoon ridiculing the royal governor may have delighted the paper-buying public, but it bought the cartoonist a ticket to the whipping post. Two, newspaper publishers who kept their political heads down struggled nonetheless because paper and ink were costly and revenue depended on subscriptions—a luxury beyond the reach of many. Shrinking subscriber bases drove most papers out of business.

To survive, publishers needed a new business model. Advertising was virtually unknown, but each new immigrant ship brought settlers anxious to establish businesses. As they opened shop, craftsmen from coopers to clothiers tried to spread the word. Ads began to appear in the backs of newspapers, providing publishers with a critical new source of revenue.

Newspapers that advertised used the new income to lower subscription costs, and with that sell more papers. Broader reach meant greater influence, which in turn allowed publishers to charge more for advertising. As customers filled their shops, tradesmen bought more ads, papers thrived, and commerce enriched the ever-expanding colonies. Before long, advertising transformed both the publishing industry and the enterprises it served until the two became interdependent.

Benjamin Franklin, one of the most successful publishers of the day, leveraged this model with particular deftness. He personally taught business leaders the fine points of print marketing. As the back pages of his *Pennsylvania Gazette* filled with ads, the paper quickly became Philadelphia's favorite. Building on this financial success, Franklin set up an intercolonial newspaper network from South Carolina to Connecticut, earning him the title Patron Saint of Advertising.[1]

Throughout this era, merchants realized that the more prominent the ad, the greater the impact, but standard newspaper practice packed most advertisements cheek by jowl in the back pages with a few between articles. Businesses experimented with size, design, font, and page placement of ads, seeking new ways to impact readers with their messages. In time, they discovered that the most effective advertising strategy was interruption, placing ads directly in readers' way as they read a story. This technique hooks the reader's interest with a news story, then interrupts midstream with a brand message. Sudden intrusion into the reader's flow of thought forces the brand's message into a consumer's consciousness.

Publishers, fearful of annoying their subscribers, resisted this tactic at first, but addicted as they were to ad income, they soon made the practice a newspaper norm, forcing readers to jump from the front page through the ads to finish a story.

With hindsight, we now realize that the instincts of those nineteenth-century newsmen were accurate—the more we interrupt consumers, the less we satisfy their overall experience. From the earliest days of advertising, the scent of annoyance has wafted between interrupt ads and interrupted context—be it news, fiction, or sports or other live events. Audiences simply learned to tolerate it.

At the end of the nineteenth century, rail lines connected cities, allowing manufacturers to reach far beyond the limits of local delivery trucks. Businesses rushed to capture rapidly expanding markets by shifting from local to regional or national campaigns. Ivory Soap was one of the first brands to launch truly nationwide advertising, with an initial ad buy of $11,000.

By 1897, surging success increased Ivory's ad budget to $300,000 and earned an estimated 20 percent national market share at its peak. Many other recognized brands quickly followed suit.

Newspapers were just the beginning. In the early twentieth century, inventor and entrepreneur Guglielmo Marconi hoped to use his patents to control all wireless communication and create a subscription model for radio. But in 1906, an international treaty signed in Berlin decreed that no person, company, or country could monopolize the radio waves. Early broadcasters, therefore, had no choice but to establish the first completely ad-supported media.[2]

When commercial television began in the 1940s, broadcasting adopted radio's interrupt advertising methods, and fast became the dominant form of media consumption. At their height, the three major networks (ABC, NBC, CBS) reached a

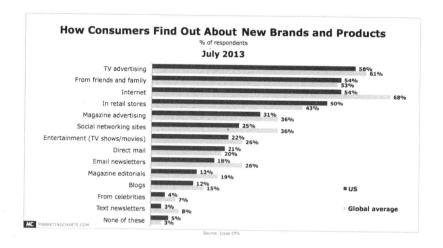

How Consumers Find Out About New Brands and Products
% of respondents
July 2013

	US	Global average
TV advertising	58%	61%
From friends and family	54%	53%
Internet	54%	68%
In retail stores	50%	43%
Magazine advertising	31%	36%
Social networking sites	25%	36%
Entertainment (TV shows/movies)	22%	26%
Direct mail	21%	20%
Email newsletters	18%	26%
Magazine editorials	13%	19%
Blogs	12%	15%
From celebrities	4%	7%
Text newsletters	3%	8%
None of these	5%	3%

MC MARKETINGCHARTS.COM

Source: Ipsos OTX

combined fifty million viewers every night during prime time. For sixty years, the television commercial was the primary way Americans learned about new products.

Television outperformed all other media because it combined mass reach, a rich visual medium for messaging, and guaranteed audience attention. Marketers poured more and more money into television advertising over time, creating increasing demand for ad inventory.

And with that spend, ad addiction grew stronger—media companies could not get enough. They began to cram more advertising into each broadcast hour to drive their revenues and profits higher. In the 1950s, advertising accounted for four minutes of viewing time per hour. By the 1970s, commercial time had doubled. But with the growth of cable TV in the 1980s and then the open Internet in the early 1990s, audiences fragmented and advertising rates for individual shows began to fall. Ad-supported networks and cable channels scrambled to protect revenues by shoving still more advertising at an ever-shrinking audience. By 2011, cable networks were running ads for almost one minute out of every three.

CONSUMERS RESIST

By 2006, however, new technologies stepped in to help consumers skip ads. The video recording device TiVo marketed its "30 second skip" feature as a key benefit. Cable providers soon launched video on demand (VOD) so subscribers could bypass ads more easily than ever. A study by the Association of National Advertisers and Forrester Research showed that marketers watched the adoption of these services with nervous pessimism. Seventy percent of advertisers surveyed thought DVRs and VOD would "reduce or destroy the effectiveness" of the traditional thirty-second ad.[3]

In 2006, *Advertising Age* predicted this: "When DVR usage reaches 30 million households in the U.S., expected within three years, almost 60% of advertisers say they will spend less on conventional TV advertising; of those, 24% will cut their TV budgets by at least 25%."

Time magazine reported that from 2009 to 2013, the average cost of a thirty-second prime-time TV commercial dropped 12.5 percent. When falling ad rates shrank revenues at ad-supported networks, they squeezed even more ads, albeit at a lower cost per ad, into their shows. In February 2015, the *Wall Street Journal* reported that cable networks were subtly speeding up the action in each broadcast hour to generate more time for ads.[4] The *Journal* quoted one studio executive as saying, "It has gotten completely out of control. Actors' performances are being seriously hurt by running shows this way."

To continue to capture ad revenue, media companies experimented with new options, shifting content onto services like YouTube so they could "pre-roll" the ads that appeared before short videos.[5] At Hulu, they fell back onto their old habits, recycling the same tired interrupt ad model that once worked on broadcast TV. Either way, marketers could at least guarantee that viewers saw their ads, because their media partners prevented fast-forwarding to skip ads.

These new capabilities, however, came with a price. By 2013, the cost of targeted online video ads had shot past that of television advertising, because pre-roll ads on YouTube and interrupt ads on Hulu guaranteed viewership and online delivery enabled more powerful ad targeting.[6]

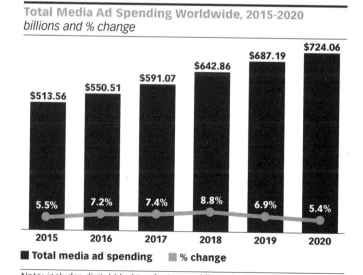

Total Media Ad Spending Worldwide, 2015-2020
billions and % change

	2015	2016	2017	2018	2019	2020
Total media ad spending	$513.56	$550.51	$591.07	$642.86	$687.19	$724.06
% change	5.5%	7.2%	7.4%	8.8%	6.9%	5.4%

■ Total media ad spending ■ % change

Note: includes digital (desktop/laptop, mobile and other internet-connected devices), directories, magazines, newspapers, out-of-home, radio and TV
Source: eMarketer, Sep 2016
216592   www.eMarketer.com

★   ★   ★

In 2016, marketers were projected to have spent a record $605 billion on advertising around the world. Digital ad spending surpassed television ad spending for the first time, as budgets continued to shift to Facebook and YouTube.[7] And advertising is projected to continue to grow, albeit at a slower pace, in 2017 as media companies, new and old, continue to work to find new ways to interrupt consumers on behalf of brand marketers, all the while denying viewers the best possible experience.[8]

But one important thing has changed.

CONSUMER'S REVOLT

Although the early Internet connected the globe and offered sufficient speed for consumers to browse and read articles, connections were not fast enough for reliable video delivery. Even short YouTube videos needed time to buffer, or they would stall during playback.

But by 2005, broadband adoption in the home surpassed dial-up in the United States. With this faster connection came a game changer for consumers: choice.

Consider Netflix, which was originally launched as a DVD subscription service in 1999, competing with Blockbuster and other video rental stores.[9] With broadband adoption now at scale, Netflix launched a fledgling streaming service in 2007, offering consumers the ability to watch a small selection of the Netflix film library on their laptops. One year later, the company launched the service on game consoles and set-top boxes that allowed people to watch Netflix easily on their living room TVs.

Early Netflix consumers loved having instant access and enjoyed watching their favorite films and, later, television series completely ad-free. They were happy to pay a simple subscription fee of about $10 per month for unlimited viewing. Netflix invested new subscription revenues to grow its library, steadily adding films and then television shows, which the company licensed from traditional media partners.

Subscriber growth soared. In the fourth quarter of 2016, Netflix surpassed 93.8 million subscribers, dwarfing the reach of broadcast and cable networks.[10] The company is expanding at an accelerating rate, adding more than two million subscribers each month in countries around the globe.

Growing subscriber revenues provides Netflix with a powerful competitive weapon. To expand and retain its subscriber base, Netflix borrowed a modus operandi from HBO and began to

Netflix on the Brink of a Major Milestone
Number of Netflix subscribers at the end of the respective period*

■ United States ■ International

Year	Total	International %	United States %
2007	7.48m		
2008	9.39m		
2009	12.27m		
2010	20.01m		
2011	23.53m		
2012	33.27m		
2013	44.35m	32%	68%
2014	57.39m	40%	60%
2015	74.76m		53%
2016	93.80m	47%	51%
Q1 '17	98.74m	49%	51%

* U.S. subscriber figures from 2007 through 2010 include DVD subscribers
@StatistaCharts Source: Netflix

statista

invest in original programming. Netflix series like *House of Cards* and *Orange Is the New Black* created rabid fans who spread word of Netflix online and off. In January 2016, the *Wall Street Journal* reported, "With...a $5 billion content budget for this year, Netflix is willing to outbid most any [sic] local TV network or streaming service."[11]

It seems simple, in hindsight. Netflix returned to the same subscription media model that drove early newspapers. But instead of succumbing to the temptation of advertising, which would have put the company's financial incentives at odds with its customers' desires, Netflix kept the two aligned. The company committed to delivering the best entertainment experience possible for its customers, and that meant not interrupting that experience with ads.

Their customers responded by shifting their viewing time to Netflix. In February 2017, CNBC reported that Netflix viewers consume 116 million hours of programming every day, completely ad-free.[12] From a marketer's perspective, that's 116 million hours each day when their customers go dark, due to Netflix alone.

Netflix inspired an industry. HBO NOW and HBO GO, over-the-top[13] services launched by HBO in 2015, drove audience viewership for *Game of Thrones* alone to over twenty-five million people in 2016.[14] Spotify had fifty million ad-free subscribers for its premium music service in March 2017, after adding twenty million subscribers in the year prior.[15] Apple signed up twenty-seven million subscribers to its ad-free music service in its first two years of operation and was adding more than one million subscribers monthly.[16] YouTube introduced an ad-free option in September 2015.

Even Netflix's rival Hulu, which launched a competitive

streaming service one year after Netflix, has seen the light. Hulu was created as a joint venture among 21st Century Fox, NBCUniversal, and Walt Disney Co. Unlike Netflix, Hulu was established to move the traditional network advertising model online. Hulu charged a lower subscription fee than Netflix and showed commercials to users before and during programming.

But by June 2015, the market had spoken. Hulu's audience numbered nine million, just 14 percent of Netflix's total audience at the time. Hulu announced it was evaluating options.

Three months later, Hulu capitulated and launched an ad-free service, for just $2 more per month. The company sent a note to former subscribers, thanking them for showing Hulu the way, and inviting them back to Hulu, this time for an ad-free experience.

Thomas,
On 07/03/14, you did something for which we'll be forever grateful - You canceled your Hulu subscription.

CBS learned a similar lesson. In November 2014, CBS launched All Access, an over-the-top subscription service that included interrupt advertising. In August 2016, the company capitulated to consumer demand and started offering an ad-free version for just $4 more per month.[17]

HITTING ROCK BOTTOM: THE DECLINE OF TRADITIONAL MEDIA

On January 22, 1996, the *New York Times* launched on the Internet, providing readers around the world with access to news the night of publication. Circulation of US newspapers fell 37 percent from 1990 to 2015 as consumers moved online, with the fastest drop in subscribers coming in 2005.[18]

By 2006, marketers recognized the trend. Over the next four years, they cut newspaper advertising spending by half,

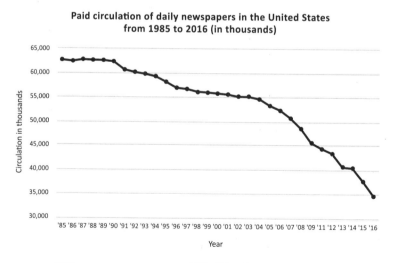

Paid circulation of daily newspapers in the United States from 1985 to 2016 (in thousands)

Source
Editor & Publisher; AAM; Pew Research Center
© Statista 2017

Additional Information
United States; Editor & Publisher; AAM; Pew Research Center
1985 to 2016

and it has continued to drop every year since. Newspapers have responded by trimming costs, sacrificing much of the content that their subscribers love.

Newspaper Ad Revenue from Digital and Print

Annual revenue in billions of U.S. dollars

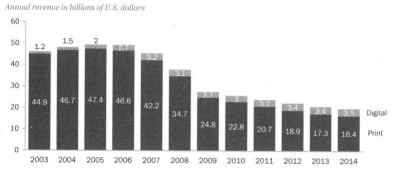

Source: Newspaper Association of America (through 2013), BIA/Kelsey (2014)

PEW RESEARCH CENTER

Slow connectivity protected broadcasters for a time. Consumers remained captive if they wanted to watch long-form programming. But today, the Netflix phenomenon is taking a heavy toll. Traditional television advertising viewership began a rapid decline in 2010.[19]

Television advertising is starting to go the way of the newspaper as marketers adapt to shrinking broadcast audiences.[20] A decline in ad spending, felt precipitously in print in 2007, began to hammer broadcast TV in 2015.[21]

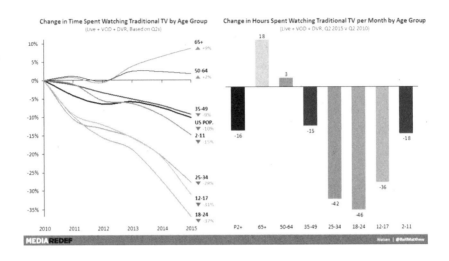

BANNER BLINDNESS AND BLOCKING

The consumer revolt against advertising is not limited to the adoption of streaming video and music services, however. Since 2008, marketers have been tracking a phenomenon called banner blindness, in which readers of a web page literally look around ads when browsing a page. Eye tracking studies, which use technology to monitor what part of a web page users actually view, initially identified the phenomenon.[22]

A study by Infolinks found that "after being asked to recall the last display ad they saw, only 14% of users could name the company, the brand, or the product, suggesting that brands are wasting millions of dollars in ads that consumers don't remember."[23]

And then the news for marketers got even worse. In September 2015, PageFair and Adobe announced that 198 million people were using ad-blocking software on their desktop devices globally. The study found that ad-blocking adoption is growing

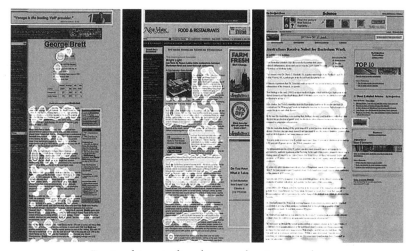

Eye tracking studies show readers ignore ads.

at 41 percent annually. One month later, Apple introduced an iOS software upgrade allowing Apple mobile devices to support ad blocking as well. The study estimated that $41.4 billion in advertisements would be blocked worldwide in 2016. A new front had opened in the popular revolt against interruption and emotional manipulation.

The rapid decline of interrupt advertising created a crisis

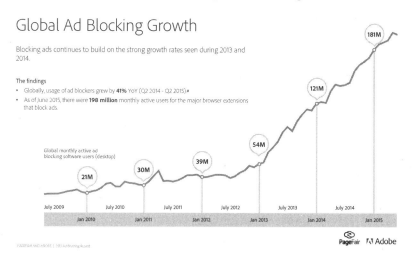

that hit media companies first. As consumers ignore, block, and pay to avoid advertising, brands have begun to cut advertising budgets. The resulting drop in ad revenues has left media business models upside down.

The second phase of the crisis will strike brands in nearly every industry. Marketers, dependent on advertising as the primary way to connect with their customers, are suddenly unable to reach them. Their brands are already starting to fade to dark, but many CMOs have yet to realize it.

THE MARKETING CRISIS

For three centuries, most companies have used the same approach to reach, acquire, and retain customers: They advertised to them. The approach was simple and consistent. Marketers identified the news and entertainment stories that their customers enjoyed most, then interrupted those stories with ads describing their products and services. By showing those ads repeatedly to customers at scale, they built growing brand awareness. If they created ads that connected emotionally with their customers, brand awareness became brand affinity.

Today's advertising crisis also created an unprecedented marketing crisis. Advertising has been a tried-and-true method to reach audiences since Ben Franklin published newspapers. As consumers block, ignore and pay to avoid advertisements, marketers must scramble to find a new way to reach their customers. Brands that fail to connect will surrender to challenger brands that discover the secret.

2

MARKETING, A STORY OF DECEPTION

Not only do consumers object to interruption, but they hate being played.

In the early decades of advertising, word of mouth traveled slowly, allowing snake oil salesmen to make false claims with impunity...until, that is, customers sickened by their cures horsewhipped them out of town.

As the telegraph and then the telephone ricocheted reputations around the country, fake goods gave way to more trustworthy products, and false claims segued into the conventional braggings and promisings that still fill contemporary ads. Today's elixirs promise whiter teeth, thinner waistlines, and fewer wrinkles, with "laboratory studies" to back them up. In short, marketing became more honest, but not so honest that today's consumers believe whatever they're told.

In a world of immediate, global information flow, exaggerated, underperforming claims backfire. Consumers compare

marketing promises with their real-world experience, and when the two don't line up, they mock the brands that played them with scathing product reviews, public tweets, and Facebook posts. Through decades of false promises, marketers have trained consumers to distrust advertising.

Don't take our word for it. Since the 1960s, comScore/ARS-group has gauged the efficacy of advertising by measuring its impact on "share of choice."[1] Today its research finds that advertising overall is rapidly losing effect, and when aimed at millennials, it's virtually useless.

THE TWO TYPES OF MARKETING DECEPTION

Historically, marketers have driven sales through two types of pretense, one rational and the other emotional. This chapter looks at each approach, why it worked in the past, and why it fails today.

1. Rational Communication

Classical marketing theory asserts this premise: Human beings are rational decision makers who, when faced with an important choice, gather relevant facts, weigh alternatives, then choose the best option. Therefore, to persuade consumers, present your claims in a factual, logical, scientific manner.

That's the theory. In reality, what advertising passes off as logic is in fact rhetoric. Rhetoric imitates science by presenting evidence and drawing a conclusion, but the difference is that science weighs all evidence, both for and against a theorem; rhetoric slants its argument by laying out only the evidence that supports its claim, while ignoring or refuting every point that contradicts it. In other words, science seeks the truth; rhetoric seeks the win. Marketing, in essence, is a public forum for rhetorical debate, a platform to persuade the consumer that one product's features outperform another's.

Ivory's classic ad executes this method to perfection. Procter & Gamble (P&G) offered a laundry soap bar that would float instead of sinking in the tub. Marketers explained the advantage in their ad: It saved time and frustration for people who otherwise would have to search around the bottom of a murky tub when they dropped a competitor's bar. Other soaps may have cleaned better (that is, after all, the purpose of soap) but Ivory, of course, never mentioned that.

Do you remember where you learned to use rhetorical persuasion? How to argue using inductive and deductive logic? Writing junior high school essays. Do you remember your seventh-grade syllogism lesson?

> "All kings are tall.
> He is a king.
> Therefore, he is tall."

In the Ivory case:

> "The best soap floats.
> Our soap floats.
> Therefore, our soap is best."

For example: Business-to-business marketers often print up a checklist of product features so the client can compare what's on offer against the competition. With never-failing regularity, the marketer's product scores tops on every feature on the list, whereas the competitor's product leaves blanks. Amazing.

As the savvy prospective buyer scans the chart, he knows two things: (1) The company self-selected only those categories in which its brand scores best. (2) Categories in which the product scored worse than the competition were left off the list.

Now more than ever, marketing via rhetorical argument provokes skepticism in the mind of the customer and a negative attitude toward your product or service.

This isn't to say that people distrust all facts, just facts used to persuade a sale. And that distrust directly affects what they are prepared to pay for what's being sold.

Dan Ariely, James B. Duke Professor of Psychology and Behavioral Economics at the Fuqua School of Business and director of the Center for Advanced Hindsight,[2] demonstrated this skepticism in an experiment with would-be stereo buyers. Ariely compared how two groups of audiophiles responded to a music system. Members of one group read what they thought was an overview by the manufacturer, and the second group read the exact same material, but believed it was by *Consumer Reports*. He writes:

> All of the participants took half an hour to listen to a composition by J. S. Bach and evaluate the stereo system. How powerful was the bass? How clear was the treble? Were the controls easy to use? Were there any sound distortions? And finally, how much would they pay for the system?

As it turned out, the participants liked the stereo much more if they were told that the information they read came from the unbiased *Consumer Reports*. They also said they would pay, on average, about $407 for the system, far more than the $282 offered by those who read the manufacturer's brochure. Mistrust of marketing rhetoric runs so deep that it colors our perception of products—even in the face of firsthand experience.[3]

If the inductive logic of rhetoric delivers suboptimized marketing results, why do businesses still gravitate toward it?

First, education. We were taught to start an essay with an opening thesis: "I'm going to prove this." Then, point by point, we'd prove it. Finally, we'd write a conclusion: "I have proved this." Today we use that same format at work. A PowerPoint presentation is just a junior high school essay with special effects.

Second, the prestige of science. Business leaders strive for scientific planning and choice making, for predictability and precision. All to the good. But in truth, business is not science. Despite access to massive sets of data, marketing decisions will always call for as much instinct as strategy. The fundamental problems never change: how to capture attention, hold it, and reward it; in short, how to turn people on, not off.

2. Emotional Communication

At the heart of an effective creative philosophy is the belief that nothing is so powerful as an insight into human nature, what compulsions drive a man, what instincts dominate his action, even though his language so often camouflages what really motivates him.

—Bill Bernbach

Post–World War II America exploded with optimism. Product debuts spiked, TV viewership skyrocketed, and the television ad fast became the most powerful way to influence consumers. But as more and more commercials jammed the airwaves, claims and counterclaims blurred consumer judgment. Which toothpaste actually brightened teeth best?

The Doyle Dane Bernbach (DDB) agency thrived because Bill Bernbach and his partners pioneered a new connection with consumers. DDB steered clients away from rhetorical praise for their product's features. Instead they set the obvious ethical questions aside and aimed powerful emotional appeals directly at the consumer's subconscious desires and needs.

According to one biography, Bernbach spoke to clients "...not of advertising, but the art of persuasion. To persuade the consumer, the creators of ads needed to touch people's basic, unchanging instincts—their 'obsessive drive to survive, to be admired, to succeed, to love, to take care of their own.' "[4]

The first step to mastering emotional manipulation is to realize that there are only two primary emotions, pleasure and pain.[5] Each, however, comes in many varieties: deeply felt positives such as happiness, peace, love, joy, as well as the sensory delights of beauty and comfort, versus profound negatives of grief, anxiety, dread, fear, loneliness, along with physical miseries that range from toothaches to migraines. In chapter 6, we'll look at how storified marketing moves a consumer's deep emotions, but for the balance of this chapter, let's focus on the surface of physical feelings.

At the sensory level, something either feels good or hurts. An appetizer may delight your taste buds or repulse them. But if experience is only sensory, why do we feel more pleasure when we look at an authentic work of art than a copy?[6] If the sensory perception were the same, why does the thrill we feel standing before van Gogh's *The Starry Night* run far deeper than the glum scrutiny of a forgery?

As Paul Bloom, professor of psychology and behavioral science at Yale, explains in his book *How Pleasure Works*, "What matters most is not the world as it appears to our senses. Rather, the enjoyment (or suffering) we get from something derives from what we think that thing is."[7] Bloom claims that we are essentialists. Our response is conditioned by our beliefs of what things really are, what their essential nature is.[8]

In 2008, researchers at Caltech studied the link between the price of wine and how much people enjoyed it. Volunteers in the study were offered wines priced at $10, $35, $45, and $90 per bottle. First they compared the $35 bottle with the $45, then the $10 bottle with the $90 bottle. Participants reported in both cases that the more expensive wines tasted better than the cheaper ones. What's more, the pleasure GAP they reported was greater when they compared the $10 and $90 bottles.

In actuality, the $10 and $90 bottles contained the exact same wine.

Previous researchers had discovered the relationship between high price and the perception of high quality and wrote it off as snobbery. But the Caltech study used an fMRI (functional magnetic resonance imaging) device to observe the volunteers' brain activity. The imaging revealed that when the participants drank what they believed to be a more expensive wine, the region of the brain linked to pleasure lit up.[9] It wasn't snobbery. They actually enjoyed greater pleasure from the wines they believed were more expensive.

The same applies to physical pain. At Harvard University, Kurt Gray and Daniel Wegner administered electric shocks to study participants. The study paired forty-eight subjects with a partner in a separate room who had the option to either play an audible tone for them or administer an electric shock.

Gray and Wegner separated the participants into two groups. In the first, participants were told that their partner had chosen to shock them, and moments later they got a jolt. In the second, the participants were told that their partner had chosen to play a tone sound, but then, as if by accident, they, too, received an electric shock. The same voltage was used in both groups.

The finding: Participants who believed they were shocked intentionally felt the shocks more painfully, and the pain lingered throughout the study. Those who believed that the shocks were unintentional experienced less pain and a quicker recovery.[10]

For both pleasure and pain, the meaning of the perception, not the sensory experience alone, determines how much pleasure or pain people experience. Because pleasure and pain are great motivators, creating these experiences within an ad promised to be marketing's most powerful tool.

Unfortunately, however, this insight devolved into the techniques of seduction and coercion. Seduction entices someone to do something with the promise of pleasure; coercion persuades them to act with the threat of pain.

Consider the ad on the following page: As you look at it, does the taste of Bud really matter? Sex sells.

Fear also sells. Political ads coerce with fear of terrorist attacks, fear of losing your job, your health care, your income. Home security companies coerce with images of burglars jimmying your windows. Tech companies turn threats of hacks, viruses, and data theft into sales.[11]

Emotion-targeted tactics have paid off since Bill Bernbach championed the "Mad Men" revolution. So why not stick with tradition?

Why not? Because today these ploys not only fail, they offend.[12] People with money to spend are savvy consumers of

media. After exposure to tens of thousands of commercials, they can smell seduction and coercion before the logo hits the screen. That's why nearly two-thirds of millennials use ad-blocking software to cut manipulators out of their lives.[13]

What's left? If emotional manipulation angers people, and if rhetorical persuasion strikes them as BS, how can you connect with your customers? How can you solve your marketing crisis?

STORY

Stories are equipment for living.

—Kenneth Burke

We advocate a solution that's tens of thousands of years old, the mode of communication that best fits the mind, that best connects one mind with another, that wraps the clarity of a rational message inside an emotional package and delivers it with sticking power: story.

A well-told story captures our attention, holds us in suspense, and pays off with a meaningful emotional experience. Emotional because we empathize with its characters; meaningful because the actions of our *protagonist* deliver insights into human nature.

The word itself, *story*, confuses many marketers. Some, for example, use the words *content* and *story* as if they were interchangeable. But as we'll discover, that's like conflating paint in a can with a masterpiece on a wall.

Many assume that because they've seen and heard a lifetime of stories, they could easily create one. But that's like thinking you can compose music because you've been to concerts.

Many hear the word *story* and imagine a tale told to children at bedtime or yarns traded over beers at a bar. Those are indeed stories, designed simply to entertain. At the other end of the spectrum, great stories have the power to change how humanity sees reality. Storified truths have built civilizations and religions that billions follow. Novels like *Uncle Tom's Cabin* created political movements that led the way to war. TV series like *All in the Family* and *Will & Grace* called out bigotry and paved the way for LGBT justice.

And as we'll demonstrate in Part 3, thanks to storified marketing, innovative brands can tell stories that change how their consumers view the world, and blow past their competition when they do.

In short, story is the ultimate I.T. *I* in that storytelling demands information—a wide and deep knowledge of human nature and its relationship with the social and physical realms. *T* in that a well-told story demands skillful execution of its inner technology, its mechanisms of action/reaction, changing value charges, roles, conflicts, *turning points*, emotional dynamics, and much more. A craft underpins the art.

Story structure, as we'll see in the next chapter, is intrinsic to the human mind. Why then do we need to learn its craft? Isn't storytelling natural? By the same token, children can sketch stick figures. Isn't drawing also natural? Yes, both are, but to achieve excellence, authors and painters move beyond instinct to experiment and master their craft anew.

After centuries of struggle, the mathematics of perspective, for example, was finally discovered by Renaissance artists seeking to perfect realism. Art schools have taught this technique ever since because if we expected young painters to discover the secrets to perspective on their own, it would take their entire careers to achieve what they can learn in a single course. Most, in fact, would never discover it.

Similarly, a form shapes story and a craft executes the telling. If you study story technique, you can learn to hook, hold, and reward your audience's attention, as do the finest of films, plays, and novels. If you refine these skills, you can build bonds of loyalty between your brand and your clients. And finally, if you master storified marketing, as did the likes of Apple, Red Bull, Dove, and GE, your brand will, like theirs, resonate around the world.

PART 2

STORY CREATION

Story: The evolutionary adaptation to consciousness

3

THE EVOLUTION
OF STORY

The target of all business strategy is the human mind, that biological engine built by evolution to constantly create and consume stories. Storified communication is not just another selling technique, but the key to capturing, engaging, and rewarding customer attention. As research has repeatedly shown, when marketing storifies its messages, consumers listen. In the age of distraction, attention caught and held is the marketer's single most valuable asset.[1]

To bring home story's unique ability to capture and hold audience attention, this chapter traces the evolution of story from day one. What follows is a speculative saga that spans hundreds of thousands of years and blends multiple scientific interpretations of human fossils[2] into a three-act adventure that begins with the birth of consciousness. It builds as the mind battles for survival, and climaxes with the triumph of storified thought.

ACT I: THE FIRST HUMAN THOUGHT

The nervous systems of billions upon billions of creatures evolved into greater and greater complexity over hundreds upon hundreds of millions of years. Then beginning two to three million years ago, severe planetary changes forced the central nervous systems of anthropoid bipeds to add brain matter, gray and white, at an average rate of one milliliter every three thousand years.[3]

The front-most portion of the prefrontal cortex known as Brodmann area 10 sits just behind the forehead. During human evolution, its six cortical layers expanded enormously in both size and reticulation, forcing the skull to grow wide and high. Over time, mutation by mutation, the hominid cerebrum gained one full liter of mass and became so tumescent, so structurally complex, its hundred billion cells so interconnected, that the brain, straining to the breaking point, erupted with the first human thought: *I am.*

The silent awareness of "Me" suddenly transformed a brain into a mind and turned an animal human. Animals react to the objects around them, but the human brain turned itself into an object. Consciousness, in effect, split itself in two.[4]

Self-awareness is like a mild schizophrenia. When you look at yourself inside yourself and think the thought *You idiot!*—who is angry with whom? When you're pleased with yourself, who pats whose back? When you talk to yourself, who listens? How do these inner transactions work?

It goes something like this: Behind your active mind, at the irreducible crux of your humanity, an awareness observes your every thought and deed. This core self is the "proprietor," so to speak, of your mind. As if looking through an inner prism, this subjective self splits off a version of itself, and then watches this doppelgänger think, choose, and act in the world. The core self then judges its outer self, positively or negatively, seeking to change its thoughts and behavior.

The core self's observation of itself, strange though it may seem, is both natural and persistent. Tonight, as you dream, you will become a self-aware audience of one, watching yourself perform in your dreams as if you were an actor in an oddly unrealistic film.

Awake, you're doing it now. If you were to ask yourself *Who am I?*, a sense of "Me" would rise up from the bedrock of your being. This awareness of "me-as-owner-of-myself" hovers behind your foreground consciousness, observing your waking thoughts, watching you read this, and noting how you're doing. Don't bother to turn and look. You cannot face yourself within yourself, but you know that "Me" is always there, always mindful, always watching.[5]

When self-awareness invaded the first human mind, it brought with it a sudden, sharp sense of isolation. The cost of self-consciousness is a life spent essentially alone, at a distance from all other living things, even your fellow human creatures. With that first, primordial *I am* moment, the mind felt not only alone but also in terror. For self-awareness brought another, even more frightening discovery, unique to humanity: time. The first human being suddenly found herself alone and adrift on the river of time.

ACT II: THE SECOND HUMAN THOUGHT

In the wake of *I am* came the second human thought:...*and someday my time in time will end*. Not long after the birth of self-awareness, time-awareness flooded the mind, bringing with it dread. Fear is an emotion we feel when we don't know what's going to happen; dread is the emotion that grips us when we know what's going to happen and there's nothing we can do to stop it. And one dread is certain: Our days will stop like an unwound watch.

Prior to self-awareness, our Pliocene ancestors, like all animals, lived in the corporeal comfort of a perpetual present. But when the sense of *I am* separated self-awareness from its primal instincts, visions of a painful future streaked through the newly minted human mind.[6] What's more, the mind discovered that not only is the future in doubt, but the surfaces of people and things cannot be trusted; that nothing is what it seems.

What *seems* is the sensory veneer of what we see, what we hear, what people say, what people do. What *is* hides beneath what seems. For truth is not what happens, but how and why what happens happens. With neither science nor religion to explain life's unseen causalities, the suddenly self-aware mind must have roiled in confusion as chaos, enigma, meaninglessness, and brevity made life unlivable. The mind had to find a way to make sense out of existence.[7]

ACT III: THE STORY-MAKING MIND

That's when story rode to the rescue. Gene by gene, natural selection implanted the mental mechanisms of story-making into our DNA. As David Buss puts it, story-making is "...an evolved psychological mechanism, a set of procedures within the organism designed to take a particular slice of information and transform it via decision rules into output that historically has helped with the solution to an adaptive problem. A psychological mechanism exists in current organisms because it led, on average, to the successful solution for that organism's ancestors of a specific adaptive problem."[8] In the case of human beings, the problem was chaos and the dread of death.

The storifying mechanisms of the mind work in this way: Throughout the day, the body absorbs millions of bits of raw, sensory stimuli. Somewhere below the level of consciousness, the mind sorts through this mass and imposes decision rules that sort the relevant from the irrelevant. It ignores 99 percent of all data and concentrates on the 1 percent that grabs attention.

And what grabs attention? Change. As long as conditions remain secure and constant, we pursue the business of life, but come change, and we're suddenly under threat or surprised by good luck. In either case, we react. Subconscious survival systems kick into gear—chief among them story-making. Instantly, the core self triggers the mind to *storify* this event.

The brain flexes its storifying muscles in Brodmann area 10. Here, the past flows into the future as the mind recalls previous events and projects possible outcomes. The mind compares prior happenings of a similar kind with its current experience, so it knows what to do now and what to do in the future should this ever happen again.[9]

The mind, of course, does not convert every trivial change to story. Instead evolution has taught us to focus on meaningful, dynamic change.

Storified thought interprets every event in terms of its core value. In story creation, however, the word *value* does not refer to mono-concepts such as success, truth, loyalty, love, or freedom. Those words name only half a value. Dynamic events affect our lives not as singularities but as binaries of positive/negative value charge. They pivot our lives around experiences of success/failure, truth/lie, loyalty/betrayal, love/hate, right/wrong, rich/poor, life/death, winning/losing, courage/cowardice, power/weakness, freedom/slavery, excitement/boredom, and many more. Values pump the lifeblood of story.

For an event to be meaningful, the mind must sense that the charge of at least one value has undergone change. The reason is obvious: If the charge of a value at stake in a situation does not change, what happens is a trivial activity of no significance. But when a value's charge changes from positive to negative or negative to positive (for instance, from love to hate or hate to love; from winning to losing or losing to winning), the event becomes meaningful and emotions flow. Because a well-told story wraps its telling around emotionally charged values, its meaning becomes marked in our memory.[10]

This is why a fictional event can be more memorable than an actual happening. Well-told stories implant patterns of possible behaviors as if they were the memories of actual experiences. These become matrices for future actions. The confused values in real life often make events forgettable, while the clarity and power of a fictional emotional charge cement it in memory as a powerful future reference point.[11]

To make sense out of life, the story-making mind strings meaning-charged events through time, connecting and unifying them by cause and effect. At story's end, meaning is not only understood rationally but also felt emotionally.

The form of story, at its simplest, goes like this: As the telling opens, the central character's life, as expressed in its core value (happiness/sadness, for example), is in relative balance. But then something happens that upsets this balance and decisively changes the core value's charge one way or the other. He could, for example, fall in love (positive) or out of love (negative). The character then acts to restore life's balance, and from that moment on a sequence of events, linked by cause and effect, moves through time, progressively and dynamically swinging the core value back and forth from positive to negative, negative to positive. At climax, the story's final event changes the core value's charge absolutely and the character's life returns to balance.

The evolving mind's mastery of storied perception gave it the means to streamline the overwhelming deluge of actuality into a manageable, efficient, human-size reality. Its story-structured processes imposed order, unity, and meaning on a chaotic, discordant, meaningless existence. Thanks to storied thought, humanity learned how to survive with purpose and balance. As Kenneth Burke put it, story equips us to live.[12]

THE EIGHT POWERS THAT PROPEL STORY

In order to storify thought, the mind evolved and perfected eight powerful faculties. When used in concert, they interconnect our impressions of people, places, and things scattered through our past, present, and future into the coherent assemblage we call reality.

1. Self-Awareness: The power to distinguish the mind's subjective, core self from its objective, public self and observe the outer self as if it were a separate personality.

Self-awareness, as we noted above, came with the first human thought. Although time changes the objective self, the core self feels that it lives unchanged and outside of time. Nonetheless, "Me" also realizes that it cannot exist without its objective self, and therefore dreads its loss.

Over time, storied thinking reshaped perception; the mind found meaning in existence and belief in life after death. With purpose in one hand and immortality in the other, humanity finally took its place in time.

2. Other-Awareness: The power to look behind the eyes of another person and sense within him a consciousness very much like your own.

With other-perception, your mind infers that whatever happens inside itself also happens inside the minds of others. Strong other-awareness becomes empathy—a combination of identification and insight such that when something happens to another person, it feels as if it happens to you.[13]

For the storyteller, other-awareness guides the creation of the characters that make the choices and take the actions that carry out the story.

3. Memory: The power to store and recall experience.

The past makes the future in this way: Memory builds an understanding of people and the world by recording patterns of experience, stacking them one on top of another by what they have in common, and then telling itself, "This is how the world works."

The mind then uses these patterns from the past in an effort to control the future by taking actions designed to make history repeat itself.[14] But often, at critical moments, our memory-based sense of probability explodes when a tried-and-true action triggers a wholly unexpected effect, leaving us feeling that when it really matters, memory betrays us.

As we will see in upcoming chapters, these violations of probability become the *turning points* that propel all stories.

4. Intelligence: The power to extract knowledge from both formal learning and everyday experience, and then apply deductive, inductive, and causal logics to reason to factual, truthful conclusions.

The finest intelligence also spots fallacies and refutes them. In storytelling, knowledge generates content—the setting and its cast of characters.

5. Imagination: The power to reshape reality into undreamed-of possibilities.

When knowledge becomes time-worn, the mind loses

energy. But even the most calcified knowledge, stirred with imagination, can renew itself, becoming flexible and life giving.

In like fashion, the same old story, told over and over, risks emptiness and boredom. So story-makers call upon imagination to give their tellings limitless variations.

6. Insight: The power to see through appearances and perceive inner causalities.

An insightful mind reads surface signs and then senses the hidden forces that move within and cause things to happen. Data, for example, only measures the outer results of what has changed; insight discovers how and why what has changed has changed.

The storyteller, as we will see, uses this keen perspective to show us a world we think we understand, but then cracks open reality to first surprise us, then deliver a rush of insight into the hows and whys of that world and its characters. A lifetime of story-driven insights civilizes human beings, builds institutions, and makes culture viable.

7. Correlation: The power to create.

The correlating mind takes two things it already knows, and then seeks a hidden connection, a third thing that joins the two in a way no one else has ever seen before. This analogical logic is the essence of creativity. The discovery of the third thing fuses two known things into something utterly new—not just an innovation or refinement, but something unexpected and unprecedented.

Throughout history, master storytellers have constantly correlated new content with new forms in previously unimagined ways. But no matter how creative and revolutionary their tellings, the best stories always make a human sense, always shine a new light into human needs and human desires.

8. Self-Expression: The power to perform.

The self-aware mind harmonizes these distinct powers to thread its way through multidimensional, multileveled, ongoing realities, piecing causes to their effects, weaving people and events into story form. Telling begins in one mind, but it ends in another. None of the mind's gifts would matter if the stories it creates could not be performed for other minds to experience.

From the earliest, talented storytellers performed three kinds of stories around the fire: action epics of hunting, combat, and survival against the elements; tales of the supernatural powers that control nature; and myths of immortality in an afterlife realm. The first became the foundation legends of civilizations, the second made sense out of time and space, and the third founded the world's religions. Together these stories taught the tribe how to live in this world and prepare for the next.

THE STORY-POWERED MIND

The mind builds stories to bridge the *gap* between itself and the universe, between itself and the past, present, and future. Story form imposes order on chaos; it penetrates the enigma of the *seems* to express the cause and effect of the *is*; it unifies events to bring meaning out of meaninglessness. Knowledge expressed in story form gathers other human beings around its themes, uniting communities and building cultures.

So, in the marketing context, the takeaway is this: Storified communication is the most powerful form of messaging because story fits the mind; story fits the mind because the mind converts actuality into story in the first place. It's a tautology. As Hamlet says, "There is nothing either good or bad, but thinking makes it so."

This is why story alone represents a way out of today's marketing crisis—once you master story's structure and how telling works.

4

THE DEFINITION OF STORY

To master storified marketing, CMOs need solid working answers to fundamental questions: "What exactly is a story? What are its primal components? How do these elements interact within a story? How do I create a powerful marketing story? How will this story create and convey the meaning I want to express? How does this story play out within my consumer's mind? Influence her feelings? Guide her choices? And most important, how will this story motivate my customer to a positive, profitable action?"

Story, like *art* and *music*, is a word you think you understand until you try to define it. You might wonder why. After all, you have heard a lifetime of stories; you can cite hundreds of examples; you tell stories every day to your friends, co-workers, and self. You assume you know what story is, and yet your definition seems ambiguous at best.

Reference books offer little help. Consider this from the *Oxford English Dictionary*: "An account of imaginary or real people and events told for entertainment." For the working marketer, a soft definition like that is beyond use. No one can work with a tool if he doesn't know what it is, what it does, and how to fix it when it breaks.

To make matters worse, *Roget's Thesaurus* runs thick with confusing metonyms like *account* and misnomers like *journey*. When a marketer mistakes one of these softer versions for the real thing, he mistakenly assumes his campaign tells a strong story when in fact it does not. As a result, the campaign fails and he blames its story, not realizing that he didn't tell one in the first place.

Let's clarify what story is by first looking at what it is not and eliminating any weak synonyms or false equivalents.

STORY IS NOT A PROCESS

Auto parts moving down an assembly line to become a car, bolt by screw by rivet, is not a story. Manufacturing is a horizontal process. Like a story, the operation has a beginning, middle, and end that moves from an open state to a closed state—in this case, from disassembled to assembled. But unlike a story, a process has neither a desire nor a conflict nor a *core character*. As a result, no one's life is touched or changed. A process accumulates; a story progresses.

STORY IS NOT A HIERARCHY

When asked to tell their company's story, many executives simply reach for its organizational chart. For them, the corporate "story" describes how things get done, how decisions and tasks flow up and down the pyramid of power. But corporate organization is simply another kind of process—in this case, a vertical one. Hierarchies supplant chaos with order but tell no story.

STORY IS NOT A CHRONOLOGY

Other executives, when asked the same question, recite their company's history. But a corporation's chronology, especially the kind found in investor prospectuses, is, once again, just another process. In this case, it's a temporal one told as a list of growth marks accumulated over a sequence of dates.

STORY IS NOT A JOURNEY

The buzzword *journey* is a fashionable false metaphor for "life story." Life, of course, is nothing like a journey. If our days have any pattern, they zigzag elliptically as we reach left and right, striving for achievement, love, and security.

Euphemisms, such as *journey*, separate the mind from the unpleasant realities around it, and, like the genteelisms we use when we toilet-train children, they have a place in polite society. But the protagonist of a well-told story is not a passive passenger; she struggles dynamically through time and space to fulfill her desire.

STORY IS NOT A NARRATIVE

Many marketing campaigns have flopped because an ad agency didn't know the difference between *narrative* and *story*. *Narrative* may sound academic, even scientific, but in a business context, the term is neither logical nor precise. Its use commits a categorical error for this reason: All stories are narratives, but not all narratives are stories. The four misnomers listed above are narratives, not stories.

Narratives tend to be flat, bland, repetitive, and boring recitations of events. They slide through the mind like juice through a goose, and as a result, they have little or no influence on customers.

Stories, on the other hand, are value-charged and progressive. The mind embraces a well-told story; the imagination is its natural home. Once through our mental door, story fits, sticks, and excites consumer choice.

The next time you're bored to the bone by somebody's "story," in all likelihood you're not being told a story. If you were, you'd be listening and engrossed. Instead the guy is torturing you with a narrative, probably a repetitious recitation of "...and then I did this and then I did that and then I did the other thing and then and then and then..."

WHAT STORY IS

What is a story, precisely? The essential core event in all stories ever told in the history of humanity can be expressed in just three words: Conflict changes life. Therefore, the prime definition becomes: a dynamic escalation of conflict-driven events that cause meaningful change in a character's life.

THE EIGHT STAGES OF STORY DESIGN

When story aspires to art, it becomes an infinitely complex and endlessly variable thing. Fiction's styles range from farce to tragedy; its compounds span from the one-man show to interweavings of dozens of plots and subplots; its lengths fluctuate from the seconds it takes to tell a joke to the hundred-hour multi-season television series. At the heart of all these variants, however, beats a minimal but essential form. When we use the phrase *story form*, we mean it's universal, irreducible foundation.

If we were to dissect every coherent story ever told, eight essential components, assembled over eight stages, would span the creative process from beginning to end:

STAGE 1	STAGE 2	STAGES 3-8
EFFECT	**SUBJECT MATTER**	**EVENT DESIGN**
Meaningful Emotional Satisfaction	Core Value Protagonist Society Place Time	Protagonist's Actions Versus Antagonistic Reactions

The performance of these elements varies as much as people vary. No two personalities are quite the same, nor are any two stories they tell. Inside each telling, however, an essential skeleton holds organs and limbs in place while it moves through time.

As with the arts of music and dance, the primary dimension

of a story is time. In the same way that classical music divides performances into movements through time, the life of a well-told story can be broken into eight stages of creative preparation and dynamic change. The success of each stage depends on the execution of its defining principle.

To illustrate each stage and the prime principle that guides it, we will use MONEYBALL (2011), a film written by Steven Zaillian and Aaron Sorkin. The Motion Picture Academy nominated the film for six Oscars, including Best Actor, Best Picture, and Best Adapted Screenplay.

STAGE ONE: THE TARGET AUDIENCE
PRIME PRINCIPLE: MEANINGFUL EMOTIONAL EFFECT

Before an author composes his story, he needs a clear vision of his audience and the final effect his work will have on both their thoughts and feelings.

MONEYBALL: The screenwriters aimed at an adult audience of sports lovers in general, baseball fans in particular, and all those who adore Brad Pitt. Since most of the true fans in the audience already knew the outcome of the events portrayed in the film, the specific rational effect the storytellers aimed for was a deep understanding of the hows and whys behind the events. Their specific target of meaningful emotional satisfaction was the calm sense of gratification that comes when a quiet hero beats the odds from behind the scenes.

STAGE TWO: SUBJECT MATTER
PRIME PRINCIPLE: BALANCE

A story takes place at a specific time in a specific physical and social world. As the telling begins, the PROTAGONIST's life is anchored in a core value that rests in a state of balance. His days contain as many minor ups as downs, but the positives and negatives of this value even out to a more or less neutral state.

MONEYBALL: The subject matter of the Zaillian and Sorkin screenplay was the true story of Billy Beane, general manager of the Oakland Athletics, and Beane's struggle to build a winning team.

In 2001, Billy Beane (Brad Pitt) put together a reasonably successful team; his A's made the playoffs, although not the World Series. The core value in Beane's career—success/failure—rests in balance.

STAGE THREE: THE INCITING INCIDENT
PRIME PRINCIPLE:
IMBALANCE

The inciting incident is an unforeseen event that starts the story by upsetting the balance of the core character's life. The neutral charge of its core value turns sharply positive or negative. Either way, this radical change puts the character under pressure.

MONEYBALL: As the 2002 season begins, Billy Beane meets Peter Brand (Jonah Hill), a Yale economics grad who introduces him to the sabermetric method for evaluating players. Beane suddenly sees the beauty in this method and hires Brand as his assistant. This inciting incident turns the balance of Beane's life sharply to the positive. He has hope for the coming year. His core value of success/failure tilts toward the upbeat.

MONEYBALL's inciting incident, however, also brings an unfortunate side effect: The moment Beane embraces the non-traditional data analysis of sabermetrics, he finds himself at war with key personnel—team manager Art Howe (Philip Seymour Hoffman) and chief scout Grady Fuson (Ken Medlock)—who hate sabermetrics. Seen from this angle, the full impact of the inciting incident pivots Beane's sense of success/failure sharply from positive to negative. He has major, career-wrecking conflicts ahead.

STAGE FOUR: THE OBJECT OF DESIRE
PRIME PRINCIPLE:
AN UNFULFILLED NEED

When the CORE CHARACTER senses that the inciting incident has thrown his life out of balance and into jeopardy, he naturally wants to set life back on an even keel. To do so, he conceives of an *object of desire*. This essential component of all stories is defined as that which the core character feels he must obtain to rebalance his life.

MONEYBALL: Billy Beane's OBJECT OF DESIRE is his team in the World Series.

STAGE FIVE: THE FIRST ACTION
PRIME PRINCIPLE:
TACTICAL CHOICE

To rebalance his life, the core character takes an action, a tactic designed to cause a positive, enabling reaction from his world that will either deliver his object of desire or at the very least move him toward it.

MONEYBALL: Beane, relying on Peter Brand's sabermetric scouting, hires castoff, overlooked players to replace the stars that left last year's team.

STAGE SIX: THE FIRST REACTION
PRIME PRINCIPLE: THE VIOLATION OF EXPECTATION

Reality suddenly violates the CORE CHARACTER's expectation. Instead of getting a helpful reaction from his world, the protagonist finds that antagonistic forces very different from and more powerful than he anticipated rise up to block the protagonist's efforts. A gap cracks open between what he subjectively thought would happen and what objectively does happen. This unforeseen reaction knocks him back even farther from his goal.

MONEYBALL: The Oakland A's lose twenty-six of their first forty-six games. Art Howe attacks sabermetrics as a failure, and against Beane's wishes, he fields the lineup he wants.

STAGE SEVEN: THE CRISIS CHOICE
PRIME PRINCIPLE: INSIGHT

Now in even greater jeopardy, the protagonist stands to lose rather than gain his object of desire. So he learns from the first reaction, and with this insight he renews his efforts and chooses a second action that's more difficult, more risky than the first, yet one he hopes will cause a positive reaction that will finally get him what he wants.

MONEYBALL: Beane trades away Howe's star first baseman to force the team manager to use Brand's sabermetric choice.

STAGE EIGHT: CLIMACTIC REACTION
PRIME PRINCIPLE: CLOSURE

In a compact story, the protagonist's second action causes a climactic reaction that matches his expectations and grants him his object of desire. This climax restores the core character's life to balance and ends the story.

MONEYBALL: Beane's sabermetrically inspired team sets an American League record of 20 wins in a row, finishing the season with a win/loss record of 103–59, a berth in the playoffs, and another chance for Beane to reach the World Series.

Eight Stages of Story Design

> Stage One: Target Audience = A Meaningful Emotional Effect
> Stage Two: Subject Matter = Balance
> Stage Three: Inciting Incident = Imbalance
> Stage Four: Object of Desire = Need
> Stage Five: First Action = Tactical Choice
> Stage Six: First Reaction = Violation of Expectation
> Stage Seven: Crisis Choice = Insight
> Stage Eight: Climactic Reaction = Closure

LONG-FORM STORIES

Prime Principle: Progressive Action/Reaction

In an extended work, Stages Seven and Eight repeat with a difference and escalate the telling, progressing to its eventual climax. Again and again, the world's reactions overturn the protagonist's expectations. The new actions he takes and the surprising effects they cause swing his struggles dynamically back and forth between positive and negative charges that build with progressive power. Reversal by reversal, violation by violation, pressure mounts to the breaking point until he makes a *crisis decision* to take a final *climactic action* that irreversibly achieves or fails to achieve his object of desire.

Escalating Story: What follows is a real-life example of escalation with numerous turning points unfolding over many years. See if you can guess the protagonist from the pattern of events—events that were well publicized at the time.

Target Audience: The general public.

Subject Matter: The retail food business.

An entrepreneur founds a profitable business with a high-quality product line and becomes its CEO.

Inciting Incident: After the founder takes early retirement, the new CEO spins the business into a downward spiral.

First Action: The founder comes back as CEO, expecting to put the company back into profit.

First Reaction: The world's economy plunges; his customers can no longer afford his product. Sales fall; profits fall.

Second Action: To cut costs, he closes 10 percent of his outlets, firing their employees and many more besides.

Second Reaction: Profits fall further, the stock price with them, and Wall Street says the company is headed for failure.

Third Action: The founder reduces his prices.

Third Reaction: His sales drop even more.

Fourth Action: He cuts operating costs.

Fourth Reaction: His margins shrink.

Fifth Action: In a flash of inspiration, he rebrands his company by taking on social causes that benefit his employees.

Fifth Reaction: Inspired by these activist missions, customers come back and spread positive word of mouth.

Sixth Action: Stockholders, seeking even greater profits, urge the CEO to cut employee benefits.

Sixth Reaction: The CEO defends employee benefits.

Seventh Action: He gives his employees even greater benefits and then uses social media to market a new branding campaign that displays his pro-employee values.

Seventh Reaction: A wave of PR success.

Eighth Action: He invents a new product.

Eighth Reaction: The product fails.

Ninth Action: Learning from his failure, he asks his customers what they want.

Ninth Reaction: They tell him.

Tenth Action: He gives them what they want.

Tenth Reaction/Climax and Closure: They give him his greatest success.

This, you might recognize, is the story of Howard Schultz and Starbucks.

Most marketing uses brief, compact stories. In the practical world of business, the brevity of advertising time, along with the high costs of creatives and production, confines marketing stories to one or two turning points.

MEANING

The eight stages of story create meaning in this way: First, at the core of all stories pulses at least one binary value—such as life/death, freedom/tyranny, success/failure, truth/lie, love/

hate, and the like. This value changes its charge from negative to positive or the reverse over the course of the telling. Examples: the movement from death to life in a tale of adventure such as *Indiana Jones*; the pivot from freedom to tyranny in a political drama such as Orwell's *1984*; the growth from failure to success in a career story such as *Moneyball*.

Second, the dynamic of cause and effect within the story's events expresses the hows and whys, the "because" of change. Examples: Indiana Jones lives to fight another day because under pressure, he is courageous, cool, and smart; Winston Smith submits to tyranny because he is vulnerable to the cruelty of Big Brother; the A's win the pennant and Billy Beane saves his career because he never loses faith in his judgment. This clear, simple statement of value plus cause expresses a story's meaning in one sentence.

Chapter 6 will demonstrate how a meaning-filled, emotion-wrapped climax moves the consumer audience to a profitable action. But to prepare for that final creative step, the next chapter will first unpack each of story's eight stages and explore their contents in full.

5

THE FULL STORY

The previous chapter took a wide-angle view of story's eight stages, so you can dissect stories into their major components. To learn fast, locate the eight stages in stories you love and watch as the deep pattern of universal story form emerges.

This chapter prepares you to craft stories of your own by taking close-ups of these stages and their various aspects. Like a composer of music, a storyteller must learn to play multifaceted instruments that ultimately harmonize and crescendo.

STAGE ONE: THE TARGET AUDIENCE
PRIME PRINCIPLE:
A MEANINGFUL EMOTIONAL EFFECT

Writers of fiction for page, stage, and screen have little difficulty imagining their story's buying public. Over a career, fine storytellers develop a keen sense of their ideal target reader/audience, along with a feel for their work's target emotional effect. Comedy writers labor for laughs; romance writers strive for tears; action writers aim for excitement; authors of psychologically complex tellings hope for correspondingly complex emotional effects. At the end of the day, the professional writer judges his quality of work not by its effect on him, but by the degree to which the effect he hoped for affects his readers or audience.

For the creators of marketing stories, however, defining the target audience is far more demanding. The next chapter will examine the multidimensional research in Stage One of the purpose-told story.

STAGE TWO: SUBJECT MATTER
PRIME PRINCIPLE: BALANCE

Powerful stories will not grow in arid ground. A setting must be prepared. So once the reader/audience is in sight, storytellers build their tales from the bottom up, starting at the foundations of their story's world, preparing for the telling step by step.

Subject matter for a story contains three major components: a physical and social setting, a protagonist, and a core value. Life offers the storyteller an infinite variety of each.

In fact, more often than not, the spark of originality that ignites an exceptional story flashes through a creative's imagination not while she daydreams, but as she sweats out the grunt work of founding her story-world and planting its setups.

World-building, therefore, is storytelling's critical second step. Strong choices made here greatly increase the possibility for success; weak choices mudslide downhill, burying the stages that follow. The weakest choices of all favor the general over the specific.

Writers hoping for a best seller want their stories to influence the largest number of readers or audience members possible, so they generalize, opting for a one-size-fits-all, rather than one-of-a-kind, world. This unfortunate step actually shrinks, rather than expands, their future audience or readership.

The mind works best when it moves from the specific to the universal—not the other way around. Consider, for example, the phrase *a piece of furniture*. As you read it, a vague image blurs your imagination and halts your thoughts because your mind has no inclination to go backward to the particular. But if I say, "A wingback Duchess chair upholstered in blood-red leather," a clear image glows in your mind. Instinctively, your imagination moves forward from this particular to the general, slotting the chair into the mental category "furniture." This applies to all aspects of a story's world, physical and social.

Therefore, the principle: The more specific the setting, the more universal the story's appeal.

With an eye to his end purpose, the storyteller must identify every element of the setup, then research each in depth to generate original choices, and finally integrate these aspects with precision. As a result, he creates a unique story-world for a telling of top-notch quality.

TIME

A story's setting encloses two dimensions of time—location and duration.

1. Location in Time

The vast majority of stories happen in the here and now of their contemporary society. Others take place in a historical setting or hypothetical future, and a few in the timeless world of fantasy.

2. Duration Through Time

Story duration refers to how much time the telling spans in the lives of its characters versus how much time it takes to tell. Telling time ranges from brief seconds on YouTube to the hundred hours, more or less, of a multiseason long-form television series. With a few exceptions, the life spanned within the telling covers far more time than the telling.

SPACE

Two dimensions structure a story's space: (1) Physical—the horizontal landscape and every object on it. (2) Social—the vertical hierarchy of a society's pyramid of power and the possibility for movement up or down.

1. Physical Location

Many stories, especially on stage or in sitcoms, play out in a single, enclosed space: a living room, for example, as family members, maps spread on the floor, argue over where to go on vacation. On the other hand, most stories told for the screen or page jump from place to place: a driveway as a family packs for a trip, their picnic on a beach, their dinner in the waterfront restaurant, and so on.

2. Social Location

Every physical setting contains a social setting as well, a cast of characters defined by demographic factors such as age, gender, income, employment, and ethnicity. What's more, this cast lives in a culture defined first and foremost by its values—its ideality versus its reality, what its citizens believe they should do versus what in fact they do.

THE CORE VALUE

The physical and social dimensions brace a story in time and place, but a setting does not become three-dimensional until the teller adds substance in the form of values.

As mentioned in chapter 3, in everyday conversation, when someone says an individual or institution has "values," he means positive qualities such as truthfulness, love, generosity, hard work, loyalty, and the like. But for the story-maker, the values he invests in his telling come not as singularities but binaries of positive/negative charge: truth/lie, love/hate, generosity/selfishness, hard work/laziness, loyalty/betrayal, life/death, courage/cowardice, hope/despair, meaningfulness/meaninglessness, maturity/immaturity, justice/injustice, and on the list goes, naming all those qualities of human experience that can shift charge dynamically from positive to negative and back again.

A telling may incorporate any number, variety, and combination of values, but it anchors its content in one irreplaceable binary—the story's core value. This value determines a story's fundamental meaning and emotion.

Suppose a story's core value is love/hate. How and why a person moves from love to hate or from hate to love gives the events meaning. As the story moves back and forth between negative and positive charges, emotions flow, not only in the characters but in the audience as well.

But if a storyteller were to extract love/hate from her characters' lives and substitute morality/immorality, this switch in core value would evolve her work from a love story to a redemption plot with all-new meanings and all-new emotions.

If a crime story were to shift its core value from justice/ injustice to life/death, it would stop being a crime story and pivot to an action tale—once again, new emotions, new meanings. If a family story were to deemphasize the value of unity/ breakup and instead emphasize maturity/immaturity in one of its children, the plot would radically change genre from domestic drama to a coming-of-age story. The core value that pulses at the heart of a story determines its specific meaning and unique emotional impact.

THE PROTAGONIST

Cast design is best imagined as a solar system of planets, satellites, and comets (supporting characters) in orbit around their sun (the story's core character, aka protagonist or hero), burning at the center. A single character usually plays this star role, but it could be a duo (such as in *Thelma and Louise*), a team (*Inglourious Basterds*), an institution (the CDC in *Contagion*), even all of humanity considered as one massive group struggling to survive (*War of the Worlds*).

When two or more characters fill this role, they act as one: All members of the group want the same thing and suffer or benefit mutually as they pursue it. Whatever happens to one, positive or negative, affects them all.

A core character must be empathetic; she or he may or may not be sympathetic. The difference between these two is this: *Sympathetic* means "likable"—an amiable, companionate person the target audience might want as friend, family, or neighbor. *Empathetic* means "like me"—an innate trait shared by both the core character and the target audience.

Sympathy is optional, empathy essential, for this reason: Audience involvement hinges on an act of personal identification. No matter how charming, attractive, and sympathetic a character may seem, an audience will not connect on good looks alone. Rather, the psychological bond of empathy only develops when an audience subconsciously identifies with a positive human quality emanating from within the character. This quality becomes the story's center of good.

THE CENTER OF GOOD

The moment a story appears in front of audience members or readers, they instantly and instinctively inspect its value-charged landscape, seeking an emotional door into the story, a place to stick their empathy. They sort the positives from the negatives, the goods from the bads, the rights from the wrongs, the things of value from the things of no value. Everyone searches for a center of good because, in his heart of hearts, everyone instinctively sees himself as good.

We all know we're flawed, perhaps in need of moral fine-tuning, but when we weigh the positive versus negative charges within, we feel that on balance we're overall good, or at least right. The worst of people believe they're justified in what they think and do. Just ask them. Therefore, all people, regardless of their humanity or lack of it, seek a positive glow somewhere in a story's world, a mooring for their empathy.

Ideally, the storyteller places this center of good within the protagonist so that a positive human quality emanates from within the core character and captures the audience's personal involvement. This empathy magnet also anchors the mirror story, which we will explain in chapter 6.

Please note: The principle of the center of good is not a call for sentimentality and Pollyanna cheerfulness. Just as too-sweet candy hurts your teeth, a too-sugary world hurts your sense of truth.[1]

LIFE BEGINS IN BALANCE

Before a story begins, its physical setting, social setting, core value, and core character rest in a state of balance. The protagonist has her daily ups and downs. Who doesn't? Nonetheless, she holds reasonable sovereignty over her existence. Until... something happens.

STAGE THREE: THE INCITING INCIDENT
PRIME PRINCIPLE: IMBALANCE

Definition: The inciting incident launches a story by upsetting the equilibrium of the protagonist's life and throwing the story's core value either positively or negatively, but decisively, out of kilter. This turning point initiates the events that follow and propels the protagonist into action.

The inciting incident could be a massive social event or a

quiet inner event—a change in national leadership or a change of mind. It could happen by accident (the protagonist wins the lottery) or by decision (he quits his job to open a new business). It could cause a positive turn (the core character is offered a big promotion) or a negative turn (he goes bankrupt). It could, as it often does, move first to the positive (the core character falls in love with a great guy) and then to the negative (only to discover he's married).

From the inciting incident on, a story's core value dynamically changes its charge over the course of the telling. In storytelling, therefore, *dynamic* means more than "active" or "forceful." It means constant change and progress caused by an alternation between the positive and negative charges of values inherent in the story's events.

From the audience's point of view, the inciting incident causes four effects: First, it captures attention. As we pointed out earlier, the mind keys on change, and the inciting incident's sudden pivot of the protagonist's life sharply focuses the audience's interest.

Second, it raises the major dramatic question, "How will this turn out?" This MDQ is very adhesive mental glue. When you think back, how many perfectly lousy stories have you sat through for no other reason than to get the answer to the nagging question: "How does this piece of dreck turn out?"

Third, when curiosity over the MDQ merges with empathy for the protagonist, a story generates the compelling magnetism known as suspense. Suspense doubles involvement. This blend of subjective identification with objective wonder magnifies a story's power tenfold.

Fourth, the instant an audience sees the protagonist's

life tilt out of balance, an image forms in their imaginations, an image of a scene they know they must see before the story can end. After a lifetime of story-going, the audience knows that once an inciting incident hits, negative forces will continually block the protagonist's actions until at crisis she finally comes face-to-face, as it were, with her story's most focused antagonistic power.

This critical confrontation is sometimes called the "obligatory scene," because having caused audience members to imagine it, the storyteller is obligated to show it to them. It would be rude not to.

STAGE FOUR: THE OBJECT OF DESIRE
PRIME PRINCIPLE: AN UNFULFILLED NEED

If an event were to throw your life out of balance, what would you want? What would any human being want? Sovereignty over existence. By throwing life out of balance, the inciting incident arouses the natural human desire to regain control and restore balance.

In the wake of this starting event, the protagonist senses a sudden, radical, possibly dangerous tilt in the ground he stands on, and so conceives of an object of desire, that which he feels he must have in order to put his life back on an even keel. This could be something physical like a hike in pay, a product innovation, or the right person to love; something situational like a job promotion, a divorce, or revenge for an injustice; or something ideational like a deeper insight into himself, a higher goal in his career, or a faith to live by. From story to story, no two objects of desire are quite the same; ideally, each is unique and specific to its tale.

Nonetheless, all stories dramatize the essential human

struggle to move life from chaos to order, from imbalance to equilibrium.

We measure the worth of the object of desire in terms of risk: the greater the risk, the greater the object's worth. What would you risk your time for? What would you risk your life for? What would you risk your soul for? The most compelling objects of desire come with the highest price tags, and the greater the object's worth, the greater the involvement. Contrariwise, watching a character pursue something of no real value is the definition of boredom.

A story shapes a character's moment-by-moment struggle, but the complexity of life winds through a labyrinth of wishes and needs. Ultimately, storytelling becomes the art of merging and organizing many streams of want into a flow of events that aims at a single object of desire.

The specific desire that focuses a character's struggle to rebalance life is greatly determined by the culture he lives in. Cultural ideals determine the foreground desires that guide a character (what he *should* want) and the background desires that limit his choices (what he *must not* want).

Each of us continuously senses the relationship between ourselves and every person we encounter in life—our safety in traffic, which table the maître d' gives us, our place in the hierarchy of co-workers, to name only three public examples. We are acutely aware of our private rapport with friends, family, and lovers. We're also attuned to our innermost self, our relative state of physical, mental, emotional, and moral well-being. What's more, we're aware of our place in the flow of time; of our experiences in the past, the knife-edge of the present, and what we hope for in the future. This complex of interwoven relationships creates foreground and background desires—the shoulds and must-nots of life.

These desires not only cement the status quo of a character's life but also temper his behavior. Background desires form the web of restraints that follow every character into every scene. These fixed desires for stability limit the character's actions, restraining what he may or may not say or do to get what he wants.

The protagonist's object of desire, however, must not be confused with his motivations. Desire answers *what* questions: What does the character consciously want? What does he subconsciously long for? Motivation answers *why* questions. Why does a character want what he wants? Why does he want his particular object of desire?

The roots of human motivation reach deep into childhood and, for that reason, are often irrational. How much and to what depth the storyteller researches the whys of the characters' motivations is up to him or her. Some obsess on it; others ignore it.

Biographers of historical figures—Charles Darwin, Eleanor Roosevelt, Picasso—devote chapter upon chapter detailing the upbringing of each, trying to document the precise childhood experiences that motivated these personages to do the great things they did.

Shakespeare, on the other hand, never mentions motivation. He gives us no idea why guilt torments the ambitious Macbeth, why jealousy consumes the regal Othello, or why the foolish King Lear trusts his daughters to look after him in his old age. These tragic souls just do the fascinating things they do while we hold our breath.

STAGE FIVE: THE FIRST ACTION
PRIME PRINCIPLE: TACTICAL CHOICE

Desire demands deeds. To rebalance life, the core character must act. As he does, the actions he takes and the reactions he gets move him either closer to or farther from his object of desire. This positive/negative dynamic propels his story to climax. For a storyteller to create unique, intriguing actions, she must turn an observant eye to human behavior and the principles that govern it. Consider, for example, these two:

Principle 1. Idiosyncratic Tactics

Every human being acts from one moment to the next on his personal sense of probability, on what he feels will probably happen when he does what he intends to do next. Each person's feel for contingency flows from the sum total of his days, awake and sleeping. Life-as-lived gives him a unique vision of how the physical, social, personal, and inner dimensions of his world work, or *should* work. Therefore, from one instant to the next, whether consciously thought through or instinctively spontaneous, guided by his sense of feasibility, he takes actions designed to cause enabling, positive reactions from people and things around him.

From his quiver of personal tactics, he draws strategic behaviors, all in an effort to move toward his desire of the moment and long-term hopes. And because, like everyone else, he is one of a kind, his sense of what will probably happen when he takes an action will also be one of a kind; therefore, his choice of tactic (exact words, gestures, facial expressions, and so on) will, in turn, be one of a kind.

In other words, all actions reflect a singular point of view.

Because everyone possesses a singular combination of genes and experience, the number of real-world points of view equals the exact number of people alive at any moment. It's this infinitude of idiosyncratic tactics that inspires storytellers to imagine unique characters, the sort found in the best-told stories, with behaviors like no one else's, behaviors that fascinate.

Principle 2. Risk Avoidance

Evolution programmed the genes of every living thing to conserve life down to the last calorie of energy, take no uncalled-for risks, and yet pursue all necessary desires. Therefore, human nature, as a part of Mother Nature, always takes the conservative, minimal, and yet sufficient action in an effort to get what it wants.

Why would a person do otherwise? Why would she expend any energy or take any risk if she can get what she wants the easier, more secure way? She won't. Nature won't allow it.

Therefore, this guiding principle: A character will never do less than she has to, nor will she ever do more than she needs to; instead, she will take the minimal, conservative, yet sufficient action that she believes will move her closer to a balanced life. Bear in mind, however, that Goldilocks's choices of less, more, and just right vary enormously from person to person.

More often than not, from day to day, moment to moment, we correctly choose which actions to take. Ninety-nine percent of our actions cause the responses we more or less expect. We hail a cab; it stops. We Google a question; Wikipedia answers it. We call a friend; he's glad to hear from us. We take action; what we expect to happen happens; we get on with our day. That's life, but never, ever story.

To create a meaningful emotional experience for his audience, the storyteller evicts all empty moments, all trivialities and banalities, and embraces those events, and only those events, that bring value-charged change.

To create value-charged change, the storyteller pits the core character's sense of probability against reality's forces of necessity. Probability is what we imagine will happen *before* we take an action; necessity is what in fact happens when we *do*. The value at stake in the core character's life changes poles when the core character's first action (rooted in his subjective sense of probability) clashes with the story-world's first reaction (rooted in reality's objective necessity).

STAGE SIX: THE FIRST REACTION
PRIME PRINCIPLE:
THE VIOLATION OF EXPECTATION

Many factors and forces underlie the first reaction, so we'll work through them one by one.

THE VIOLATION OF EXPECTATION

When a character's world suddenly reacts differently and/or more powerfully than he imagined, this violation of expectation delivers a jolt of surprise, followed by a rush of insight. The clash between what he thinks will happen and the result he actually gets jolts him and splits open his reality. The character stares, as it were, into the gap between his subjective anticipation and its objective result. Then with a rush of insight, he suddenly glimpses how his world *actually* works; how its unforeseen forces of antagonism now block his path.

The phrase *forces of antagonism* does not necessarily name a villain, per se. Villains inhabit certain genres, and in his proper place an archvillain, such as the Terminator, can be a wonderful antagonist. Rather, *forces of antagonism* simply refers to the various negative obstacles that arise out of any conflict, corporeal or situational.

When an unanticipated, even contradictory, obstacle violates a protagonist's expectations, it moves him farther from his object of desire than he was before he acted. He now realizes that he cannot get what he wants the easy way. The force(s) of antagonism may come from any one or any combination of reality's four tiers: physical, social, personal, and inner. Each of these tiers may conceal a host of obstacles.

1. Physical Obstacles: The titanic forces of time, space, and every object in the natural and human-made universe: not enough time to get something done; too far to go to get something; nature's tumults from tornadoes to viruses; dark and dangerous city streets; the damn car that won't start.

To these realistic forces, fantasy genres add supernatural and magical forces of amazing variety and unlimited imaginings.

2. Social Obstacles: The powerful forces of institutions and the individuals within them.

These include all levels of government and their international, national, or local legal systems; corporations; religious organizations; schools; hospitals; the military; and even charities.

Every institution everywhere shapes itself into a pyramid of power: The people at the top have great power; the people at the bottom have little or none; the people in between have some. How do you gain it? Lose it? Go up and down the pyramid? A host of causes influences movement through these social ranks—education, personality, willpower, and, all too often, luck.

3. Personal Obstacles: The forces of pleasure and pain that arise from the intimate and often problematic relationships among family, friends, and lovers.

These range from lovemaking to divorce, from gift giving to squabbles over money.

4. Inner Obstacles: Contradictory forces within a character's body, emotions, and mind with its warring conscious and subconscious desires.

How to cope when your memory betrays you, your body breaks down, or emotions overwhelm common sense? Anxiety, for example, may swing a character's inner barometer of success back and forth between high pressure and low pressure, even though outwardly nothing in his career actually changes.

TURNING POINTS

To *turn* a scene means to change its value charge; the phrase *turning point* names the precise moment when an unforeseen force of antagonism violates expectations and pivots the value at stake from positive to negative or negative to positive. Turning points trigger change in only one of two ways—either by a direct action followed by the reaction it sparks, or by a revelation of a secret or previously unknown fact and the response it unleashes.

Ideally, every scene, in one direction or the other, veers around a turning point. Those that do not are nonevents—activity without change. Too many nonevents in a row and a story collapses into tedium. On the other hand, persistent, progressive change holds us like a tool maker's vise.

Turning points simultaneously merge the rational and emotional sides of life. To understand this twin effect, we need to examine the two sides separately.

The Rational Effects of TURNING POINTS

A violation of expectation is, in essence, an effect with an unknown cause. As a result, turning points pop questions into the mind such as "Why have things taken this unforeseen turn? Why didn't the character see this coming? Why didn't I? What caused this startling twist?"

A turning point punches a hole in reality. Curiosity compels the audience members to fill the hole with knowledge, so their thoughts rush back through previous scenes and images, looking for an unseen cause, trying to solve the mystery of "Why?" The answer has been planted beneath the story's setups. The moment the audience glimpses this hidden truth, it erupts with an "Oh, yeah, now I get it!" insight that both delights and enlightens.

For example: In *Moneyball*, when General Manager Billy Beane presents his new sabermetrics project to his chief scout and team manager, he expects that his employees will be as excited by its potential as he is. **Turning point:** The two men hate it on sight, refuse to implement it, and fight against it tooth and claw. Our eyebrows go up in surprise and we wonder why. Then with a rush of insight, we suddenly realize that the game of baseball is, after all, a nineteenth-century invention. Men who have worked and played in its traditions all their lives are not going to turn twenty-first-century without a fight.

Having hit this negative floor, the story moves off in a new direction as Billy's tactics pull them, kicking and screaming, into the modern age, driving the film to a positive climax. Along the way, *Moneyball* rewards its audience for paying attention by giving them insights into baseball history, modern baseball's methods, and the inner truths of its characters.

As Aristotle observed, the deepest audience pleasure is learning without being taught. When a tale dramatizes its meaning skillfully, the audience feels no mental strain and yet comes away with a fuller understanding of the workings of the world and the human heart.

The Emotional Effects of TURNING POINTS

Emotions begin as reactions to stimuli. When sights and sounds, tastes and touches strike the senses, the mind instantly analyzes their meanings, sorting the positive from the negative: helpful versus hurtful, familiar versus strange, beautiful versus ugly, for me versus against me, and the like.

The mind's ranking process keys on the potential for change. So long as life's conditions run in neutral, the mind pays no attention and goes about its many tasks. But when things change, awareness snaps to alert as our animal instincts warn us that change threatens survival.

Once the mind determines whether the change leans toward the positive or the negative, certain glands open and pour a cocktail of substances into the bloodstream. These infusions of chemicals we experience as *emotions*. As mentioned in chapter 2, at the most basic level we feel just two, pleasure and pain, but with degrees, variations, and complexities of each. This is why two people may have two very different responses to the same stimulus. This is also why one person may interpret a stimulus in two divergent ways and experience so-called *mixed emotions*.

Emotion, therefore, is the side effect of change. When the mind senses change from negative to positive, it releases pleasure-giving chemicals; if the mind registers a movement from positive to negative, it unleashes a painful flow.

When applied to storytelling, this phenomenon inspires the dynamic design of turning points. Consider, for example, this work by Unilever's Dove brand.

THE DOVE "REAL BEAUTY" CAMPAIGN

Ad Age named "Real Beauty" one of the top five ad campaigns of the century. It began when market researchers at Ogilvy & Mather found that only 2 percent of women saw themselves as beautiful, while 98 percent found fault, many to an unrealistic extreme. So Unilever launched the campaign in 2004 with a mission to persuade women of their natural beauty.

In 2013, Hugo Veiga created a video titled *Dove Real Beauty Sketches*.[2] The story follows a group of women who volunteer for an odd experiment: They agree to have their portrait done by a sketch artist who cannot see them. Instead they will simply tell him what they look like. This act of courage immediately draws empathy from the audience.

When the artist finishes their portraits, he does a second set of drawings, this time taken from first impressions of these women as reported by people who met them that day. Set side by side, the sketches based on the strangers' observations are clearly more attractive and true-to-life than the women's hyper-critical self-depictions. When each woman is then shown her two portraits, the difference moves her to tears.

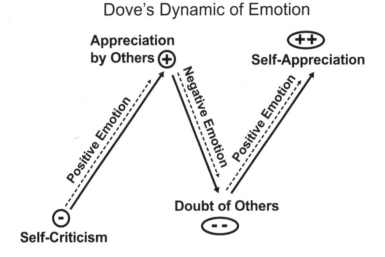

Dove's Dynamic of Emotion

THE DYNAMICS OF EMOTION

The above graphic tracks the emotional dynamics in the *Dove Real Beauty Sketches* video. Its turning points swivel between the opposing poles of its core value, from self-criticism to self-appreciation.

The story goes like this: Each woman, having consented to the blind sketch experiment, describes herself in rather unflat-tering terms (*inciting incident*). These acts of self-criticism upset the balance of their lives, turning their emotional state from neutral to negative.

But then the dynamic swings up to the positive when the women view complimentary sketches of themselves inspired by the impressions they made on strangers. They smile with pleasure (*first action*). This turning point moves the story from self-criticism (*negative*) to appreciation by others (*positive*).

But as each woman's eyes move back and forth between the two contrasting portraits, she reacts against the positive opinions of others and falls into doubt (*crisis*). Can she trust a stranger? Who should she believe? Herself or other people? This turning point takes the women from appreciation by others (*positive*) to doubt of others (*doubly negative*) and draws a corresponding negative emotion from the audience.

Then each woman's wish to believe struggles against her inner obstacle of self-doubt (*second action*) until her better nature finally wins out and convinces her to see herself as others see her (*second reaction*). The story climaxes on the doubly positive charge of self-appreciation. During this decisive transition, the audience shares in the women's triumph over self-criticism and feels, with them, a positive emotion.

All well-told stories express how and why life changes, and, as we noted above, the side effect of change is emotion. These feelings, however, only come to life during a transition. As a story shifts from positive to negative, the audience feels a dark emotion; as it transitions from negative to positive, a light emotion fills them. Once change completes itself, however, emotion quickly dissipates, ready to move in a new direction. To grip and hold emotional involvement, a story's values must transition dynamically from change to change to change. For without change, events, no matter how cheerful and energetic, dissolve into an emotionless, boring recitation of "... and then and then and then ..."

STAGE SEVEN: THE CRISIS CHOICE
PRIME PRINCIPLE: INSIGHT

The protagonist pursues her object of desire action by action, turning point by turning point, until a moment arrives near the end of the telling when the most sharply focused conflicting forces in her life now block her path. This is the obligatory scene the audience has been waiting for. At this crisis point, she has exhausted all possible tactics, save one. This powerful moment calls for a major decision. Faced with an array of possible actions, she must choose one last tactic in a final effort to put life back in balance.

THE NATURE OF CHOICE

Decisions come in two kinds: clear choices versus dilemmas—the easy versus the hard.

The *clear choice* poses a positive versus a negative option, and is, therefore, easy because, in essence, it makes the choice for you. Clear choices obey nature's grand imperative: *Always choose the positive.*

Every living thing, flora and fauna, instinctively heeds the two laws governing the conservation of energy and life: (1) Never do anything you don't have to do if you can get what you want the easier way. (2) Never take any risk you don't have to take if you can get what you want the safer way. Putting these two together, the law of nature becomes: When faced with a positive-versus-negative choice, always choose the positive over the negative, the right over the wrong, the good over the evil.

In practice, however, people rarely make choices for purely

rational reasons. The laws of nature are subject to point of view and the subjective, often irrational biases that come with it.

For that reason, once we understand that every person chooses the positive and only the positive as he subjectively sees it, and at the same time witness the tsunamis of evil that sweep through our world, we have to step back in awe of the human mind. The brain is a rationalizing wonder, a machine built to protect its own survival by turning negatives into positives.

Dilemmas also come in two kinds, and both are hard because they pose a choice between either two positives or two negatives, known respectively as *irreconcilable goods* and *the lesser of two evils*.

In the first dilemma, the protagonist must choose between two goods; she wants both but circumstances force her to choose only one. In the second dilemma, she must choose between two bads; she wants neither but circumstances force her to choose one. The hard choice of dilemma causes anxiety before the choice and risk during it. Whichever way the protagonist chooses, she stands to lose something of value in order to gain something of value: A price must be paid.[3]

In an author's fiction-told work, the crisis decision puts the protagonist under stress-filled pressure as she faces one of these two dilemmas. But as we'll see in the next chapter, in the marketer's purpose-told story, the protagonist's climactic choice must be pressure- and stress-free.

STAGE EIGHT: THE CLIMACTIC REACTION
PRIME PRINCIPLE: CLOSURE

Her strategy works. At climax, the protagonist's final choice of action causes the reaction she hoped for. She gets what she wants and needs as her world delivers her object of desire and restores her life to an even more perfect balance than when the story began. The story achieves closure—all questions answered, all emotion satisfied.

THE PRINCIPLE OF PROGRESSION

If a story's events multiply beyond the single turning point outlined above, and into a full-length (the one to two-plus hours of a film or play) or even long-form (the five-hundred-page novel or multiseason television series) story, then the principle of progression shapes the telling.

In these cases, turning points flow in a series that repeatedly and progressively moves the protagonist either farther from (negative) or closer to (positive) her object of desire, as the telling builds toward its climax and the final satisfaction of the protagonist's need. Over the dynamic of full-length and long-form stories, forces from the various levels of antagonism amplify in power and focus, deepening and widening the telling. As complications intensify, the PROTAGONIST reacts by digging deeper into her willpower as well as her mental, emotional, and physical capacities in an ever-escalating effort to restore life's balance.

The scenes not only move dynamically across the positive/negative charges of the story's values, but also arc along a progression of conflict-filled risk. The protagonist stands to lose more and more in her quest for her object of desire. As the character's struggles progress, the forces of antagonism build, calling on greater and greater capacities from within her, generating greater and greater risk and jeopardy, demanding greater and greater willpower to make more and more demanding decisions. And so on down the line to the end of the line, the ultimate climax.

As a model of this grand structure, consider the eighty-six-episode, internationally renowned AMC series, *Breaking Bad*:

In the story's first hour, the protagonist, Walter White (a guy who never smoked), discovers he has terminal lung cancer. With time running out to provide for his family, he uses superior technical know-how to create a start-up company that makes a boutique product better than the competition. Not an easy task in the face of unreliable partners and ruthless competitors.

Walter is constantly beset by raw-material shortages, on one hand, and supply-chain blockages, on the other. Plus, that bane of all entrepreneurs: government regulation. In Walter's case, the US Drug Enforcement Agency.

Like most self-made men, Walter must contend with people who feel threatened by his brilliance and cannot grasp his vision.

As he builds his business empire, he suffers major setbacks on the personal level as well. He copes with his wife's infidelity, all the while outmaneuvering his DEA agent brother-in-law. Greater and greater risks test his willpower; more and more satisfying rewards drive him on. By the series climax, Walter provides handsomely for his family, saves his partner's life, and destroys his most powerful enemy.

The next chapter adapts story's eight stages to the purpose-told story. Future chapters will harness story's pulling power to speed marketing's multiple missions.

6

THE PURPOSE-TOLD STORY

The two previous chapters laid out the underlying event design of every tale ever told, from prehistoric myths to twenty-first-century TV series. This chapter applies that ancient form to marketing's innovative twenty-first-century counterpart, the purpose-told story. Let's begin by comparing fiction-told with purpose-told, focusing on the latter's unique components.

STORYTELLING: FICTION-TOLD VERSUS PURPOSE-TOLD

Long Form Versus Short Form

The first storytellers set the standard performance length when they gathered their tribe around the fire. They geared their tales to the *single seating*—the length of time people are comfortable sitting in one place, focusing their thoughts with uninterrupted concentration. This practice became the traditional two-hour playing time (more or less) for a play, opera, ballet, or film.

Rarities, such as Neil Oram's twenty-four-hour-long play *The Warp* (see Guinness World Records), aside, the single-seating principle also explains why the writers of prose and long-form television break their massive works, such as *War and Peace* and *The Sopranos*, into units of absorption known as chapters and episodes.

Unlike full-length fictions, purpose-told stories abbreviate events. The typical business story is a mini-tale told in a thirty-second commercial or a three-minute YouTube video. GE's "Owen" ads and the *Dove Real Beauty Sketches* are two perfect examples of each.

When measured by turning points, the multiple story lines of full-length fiction pivot hundreds of moment-by-moment reversals. The marketing story, no. Purpose-told works crack open the gap between expectation and result usually only once, perhaps twice, maybe three times at the most.

General Versus Detailed Memory

Story sticks. As noted previously, the mind is a story-making, story-storing machine. As a result, stories lodge and live in memory far longer and more vividly than facts and numbers. However, the magnitude of most fiction-told stories is so great that audiences remember only the outlines of their plots and the impressions made by certain characters. Thousands and thousands of pinpointed details are foggy at best or lost altogether.

The compressed brevity of the purpose-told story makes it memorable—the most important detail being the name at the heart of a branding story or demand-generation tale. Like a favorite tune that reprises in a listener's head through the day, the purpose-told story replays itself whenever the consumer's thoughts drift toward the need for that kind of product or service.

Satisfaction Versus Action

A fiction-told story wraps a tight circle of involvement around its audience; the purpose-told story breaks that circle. Both modes begin by hooking curiosity and empathy (inciting incident), then deepening that connection through the middle (progressive complication); but when it's time to pay off (crisis/climax), the fiction-told story completes the audience's experience, while the purpose-told story extends it one critical step beyond. The purpose-told's audience members take their storified experience into the real world and relive it each and every time they purchase the subject product or service. In other words, the purpose of the purpose-told story is to transform the aesthetic pleasure of a story's climax into a viable action in the marketplace—to turn audiences into consumers.

The best purpose-told and fiction-told stories satisfy with a meaningful, emotional experience. We laugh at something we never thought funny before; we cry over something we never thought tragic before; and most important, in both cases, we gain an insight into life we never knew before, all enveloped in emotions we never felt quite that way before. This fusion of idea and emotion adds a measure of enrichment, great or small, to our inner life. We exit a beautifully told story a fuller human being than when we entered.

Single Versus Repeated Experience

But the key difference is this: The fiction-told story fulfills itself in one telling, whereas the purpose-told story retells its tale in the mind of the consumer each and every time she buys its product or hires its service. The purpose-told story moves the consumer not only to make a first choice, but to buy again and again—and what's more, to pay full price, thus building margin.

Concentrated experiences entertain because they carry us through time unaware of the passage of time. Our sense of time is so subjective that playing a musical instrument, watching a favorite sports team, competing in a video game, or immersing ourselves in a superbly told fiction makes time vanish. The story power of a fine play, novel, film, or TV series sweeps us through time until the entertainment spell suddenly breaks and we glance at our watch in amazed wonder: "Wow, was that three hours?" Some story-goers plunge back into a much-loved classic for a second, third, or more reliving. Nonetheless, the climax of each re-experience sends the fan back into daily reality.

The market-purposed story also captures the mind and erases time; it too can repeat itself into the future without limit. The public repetition of a purpose-told story becomes the chain-reactive fission known as word of mouth. The same sort of thing happens with fiction-told stories, but the difference is that (with exceptions like *Star Wars*) most titles have a shorter life span than most brands.

Author Loyalty Versus Brand Loyalty

The only loyalty the reader of a fiction-told story owes is to the author who wrote it, in the hope that the novelist's next book will deliver that pleasure again. The audience of the purpose-told story, on the other hand, ignores the artist and feels brand loyalty instead. Brand loyalty, and the lifetime of purchases that comes with it, is created by the mirror experience at the heart of the purpose-told story.

THE MIRROR EXPERIENCE

Well-told stories create two simultaneous experiences that mirror each other: one mental, the other emotional.

The mental mirror experience begins and ends with curiosity. A story's inciting incident teases the audience's mind with unanswered questions such as "What's going to happen next? What'll happen after that? How will this story turn out? Will the protagonist win his object of desire?" The rational mirror experience in story mirrors the same set of concerns and questions we ask of our everyday life. As Shakespeare said, a story holds a mirror up to nature.

The emotional mirror experience begins and ends with empathy. When a story's protagonist radiates a positive human glow from within, this center of good attracts the customer's natural instinct to connect with a fellow human being. She quickly falls into a subconscious identification, aka empathy, with the protagonist. As discussed in the previous chapter, empathy is imperative in the purpose-told story because without this essential human link, no story moves anyone to take action of any kind, let alone make a purchase.[1]

The emotional mirror experience of a fiction-told story takes two steps. The purpose-told story adds a third.

First, the *identification*. The moment the target consumer recognizes a shared humanity between herself and the protagonist, her instincts follow the logic of kinship: "That character is a human being like me. Therefore, I want that character to get what he wants, because if I were that character in that situation, I would want the same thing for myself." In other words, she bonds.[2]

Second, the *subconscious switch*. Once the target audience identifies with the protagonist, she senses that this is *her* story, and so she substitutes his storified desire for her real-life desire. By rooting for the protagonist to obtain his object of desire in the story, the audience member vicariously roots for her own desire in life.

She instinctively experiences the events *as if* they were happening to her. As the story arcs, she feels a change from negative to positive, from problem to solution, until the upending climax delivers a vicarious fulfillment of her need.

This subconscious switch from fictional to personal explains in a nutshell how and why the well-told, purpose-told story delivers results with staying power.

Third, the *reenactment*. The consumer's mirror experience motivates her to act. Wishing to relive the positive charge of the purpose-told story, she purchases the product or hires the service embedded in the telling. Her post-story reenactment satisfies her need and the marketer's purpose simultaneously. In short, she becomes a customer.

THE SCIENCE

To understand exactly how the mirror experience happens and why it works, let's step back and take another look at the neuroscience of story.

As noted in chapter 3, the brain's largest mass, Brodmann area 10, performs the executive functions of memory recall, reasoning, problem solving, choice making, and action planning. Other brain areas carry out these decisions, but the consciousness buck stops here; in BA10 the past flows into the future.[3]

The mind memorizes the patterns of cause and effect that underlie real-life past events so it can strategize its future actions. As events impact us over the years, we gather knowledge of how things work, how the various forces in our world interconnect. When new situations arise, the mind draws on these past patterns to imagine the possible tactics it might take and predict the probable reactions these actions might cause.

This process of linking previous encounters to future outcomes underlies not only factual but also fictional experience. When a story engages the mind, its virtual events play out in the theater of BA10. Memory then stows these ostensible events in an "as if" state alongside real-life events. In time, however, their as-if-ness dissipates. When preparing for the future, the mind doesn't bother to distinguish between fictive and factual events; rather, it focuses on their mutual substructures. The mind abstracts the patterns of causality that underpin both the "is" and the "as if" and merges them. This accumulated knowledge of cause and effect sets the stage for future choices.

Each person acts on her unique sense of probability, what her sum total of personal experience, actual and fictional, tells her will probably happen when she chooses to act. Through this uniquely human process, stories provide a vital source of insight and a guide from one action to the next, constructing part of the reference framework she will use to make future decisions. Wise marketers leverage this propensity with the purpose-told stories they tell.

The Eight Stages of Story Design

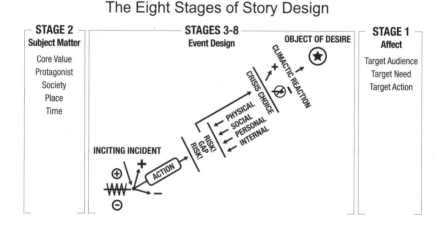

CREATING THE PURPOSE-TOLD STORY

The creation of a purpose-told story moves through the same eight stages as the fiction-told story but with an eye to creating a mirror experience that moves the consumer to a profitable reenactment. The arc of the purpose-told story guides the consumer from an absence in her life to its fulfillment, from need to satisfaction.

STAGE ONE: THE THREE TARGETS

As outlined in chapter 4, the first stage of story design identifies its targets. Authors of fiction-told tales tend to make broad assumptions about their audience, but not the creator of a purpose-told story. You, the marketer, must know exactly where you're aiming, and that means defining the target market/audience, the target need, and, above all, the end result: the target action.

The Eight Stages of Story Design

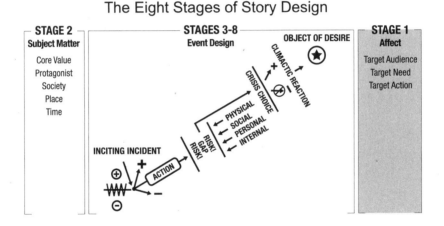

Step 1: Research Target Audience

In this big data era, the demographics of a target market (the age, gender, education, income, et cetera of the consumer, client, investor) are usually well known—and if not, then easily researched.

Step 2: Define Need/Want/Problem

What awaits discovery is the deep need harbored in the customer's secret self. Big data tells us who people seem to be, but not who they really are; surveys tell us what they keep on their shelves, but not what they keep in their hearts.

To set up the most effective, most powerful marketing story, take a major step beyond demographics and ask that classic advertiser's question: "Where does it hurt?"

This was the true genius of Steve Jobs. He saw what no one else saw: Computers were ugly. He called Dell's products "un-innovative beige boxes."[4] And he was right. It hurt just to look at Dell's wire-sprouting, cumbersome plastic cartons, let alone pick one up and carry it around. Jobs sensed what consumers subconsciously wanted but didn't consciously realize: a unique identity. To see themselves as rebellious, creative, and elite. So he made machines that symbolized those qualities with beauty, touch, and grace as they move from room to room, desk to pocket. Jobs's dream of mobile phones spoke to the unspoken needs of the consumer. Apple storified his vision in a series of brilliant commercials, and the rest is branding history.

To find your story's target need, ask, "What is my customer's pain? What does she need but not know? What hidden problem cries out for solution?"

Step 3: Design Target Action

No matter how popular a marketing story might become, it matters little if the public enjoys it like a piece of fiction and then drops it from mind. The storytelling in *Dove Real Beauty Sketches* moved people deeply, and with that, they ran to the store to buy bars of Dove soap in unprecedented numbers.

Consider what specific action you want your audience to

take. If you're telling story B2B, you may want your client to sign a contract. If your telling is B2C, you might want your customers to pick up an over-the-counter item. If you broker big-ticket items, you might want customers to visit the showroom so your sales team can do their thing. If you offer a professional service, you may want consumers to visit your website and make an appointment. If you run a branding campaign, the target action takes place in the mind of the audience member, as she goes from brand-ignorant to brand aware, or, if necessary, changes her perception from negative to positive.

Although these targets seem obvious, many promotions miss them by a mile. They don't bother to define a purpose; instead they brag, they promise, they beg "Buy now!"

STAGE TWO: SUBJECT MATTER

Preparing subject matter for the story to come takes three major steps.

The Eight Stages of Story Design

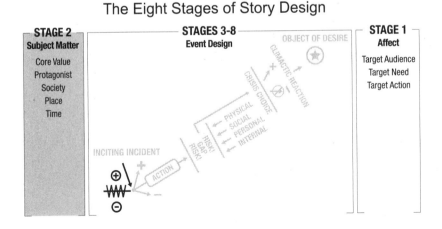

Step 1: Discovery of the Core Value

Identifying the consumer's unfulfilled need in Stage One leads to the first step of Stage Two: identifying the core value that best dramatizes the solution to this problem, the cure to this pain. Consider, for example, the storified marketing campaign that saved a brand from virtual extinction, "Real Beauty" by Dove.

As we demonstrated in the emotion-creation section of the previous chapter, this insight into the target audience's inciting incident and resulting object of desire inspired Ogilvy & Mather to weave a purpose-told story around the core value of self-criticism versus self-appreciation. Their three-minute marketing video titled *Dove Real Beauty Sketches* premiered on April 14, 2013. The dynamic of this core value and the story that expressed it connected so well with Dove's audience that the YouTube feedback was 97.6 percent positive. The video went viral with more than fifteen million views inside a week; thirty million in less than ten days. In two months it triggered 163 million global views and won the Titanium Grand Prix at the Cannes Festival of Creativity. Overall, it scored 4.6 billion media impressions and nearly doubled its sales.[5]

Step 2: Choice of Protagonist

All enterprises can be grouped into one of three grand categories depending on their essential function: *resource exploitation, product creation,* or *service performance.* Although some practice all three, each company takes its true identity from the one task it would never outsource. Marketing campaigns, by tradition, have always strived to express the unique nature of their company's brand. Therefore, marketers have traditionally cast their protagonists in sync with that one-of-a-kind identity. As a result, marketing stories tend to star one of three very different kinds of protagonists, depending on the company's core function.

1. The Resource-Centric Company

A resource-centric company beats its competition by exploiting a natural resource or raw material with greater efficiency and creativity than its competitors. Mining companies, for example, unearth the planet's minerals, while pharmaceuticals transform its biology and chemistry. Once the mineral is out of the ground or a biological secret discovered, resource-centric companies have a monopoly on their asset and therefore tend to dominate their market. What's more, the end user seems virtually invisible, sitting somewhere at the end of many distant future steps in manufacturing, packaging, and sales. In such cases, B2B marketing makes the company itself the protagonist of any story told about it.

No easy task. Reducing a corporate giant to a personality is like squeezing all fifty of the United States into Uncle Sam. It can be done, but it demands a brilliant creative leap.

2. The Product-Centric Company

A product-centric company triumphs over its competition by creating a better-functioning, better-looking, more convenient, more durable product. In this category, marketing stories often cast the product as the core character, personified as a voice, personality, or archetype. Apple's "Get a Mac" campaign, for example, starred Justin Long as an honest, commonsensical Mac computer versus John Hodgman's deceitful, bumbling PC. Or in another example, an animated Mr. Clean stars as a neo-Hercules or unbottled genie who quick-fixes Procter & Gamble's housekeeping problem/solution stories.

3. The Service-Centric Company

A service-centric company outperforms its competition by providing superior service. When it does, the end user of its medical, financial, or legal services comes out healthier, wealthier, safer. Service pros devote their talents and skills to making life better for the consumer. Marketing tradition therefore portrays the professional as the facilitator, not the hero, and instead casts the consumer as the core character. The same applies to nonprofits such as nongovernmental organizations, charities, and all branches of government.

These three casting strategies served as guidelines for marketing stories throughout the last century. But then came the rise of the Internet. When shoppers went online to rate retailers—sometimes thanking them, often denouncing them—everything changed. Word of mouth became instantaneous and viral, making consumer-centricity the mantra of modern marketing. Today campaign after campaign characterizes corporate clients as service enterprises (whether they are or not) and casts their customers as protagonists.

All good. Consumer-centric storytelling marks a positive evolution in world commerce—so long as the tellings are creatively compelling, pander-free, and, most important, honest. Millennial and Generation Z consumers detest BS.

The Empathy Imperative

If your target audience member does not sense a mutual humanity between herself and your story's core character, she will not care, not listen, not identify, not be moved to act. Empathy is absolute. This principle should be self-evident, yet rather than rewrite an uninspired story, marketers often call upon this classic rationalization: "No matter how trite the story may be, if its core character looks and sounds like the typical buyer, then emotional involvement clicks in automatically. Therefore, the cure to banality is casting." This logic, as painful experience teaches, is fallacious. An everywoman protagonist is no guarantee of customer-centricity. What the consumer wants is a human affinity, not a clichéd facsimile.[6]

In fact, for many business stories, the only logical choice for protagonist is a product or a corporation. If so, the tale must be told from that point of view. To do so, however, the storyteller faces this challenging problem: How can I fuse an empathetic connection between consumer and protagonist when the latter is either an inanimate object or an impersonal institution?

Product Identification

A protagonist, by definition, must be able to choose with a free will. A product, however, is a thing, and things have no self-awareness, no willpower, and therefore cannot make choices or take actions. The common solution calls on fantasy. Either an actor or an animated character personifies the product, or an Oz-like world brings things to life. Recent campaigns for Pier 1, Nest Labs, and Geico Insurance feature talkative teapots, chatty suburban homes, and an irrepressible Australian reptile.

Fantasy worlds and characters demand imagination, innovation, and creative execution. Rather than face that task, many campaigns abandon storytelling in favor of a spokesperson bragging and making promises the product's performance may or may not be able to keep.

Corporate Identification

As set out in the previous chapter, a demonstrably human quality deep within a core character embodies the story's center of good, its magnet for empathy. To turn a corporation into an empathetic protagonist, the marketer first must identify the company's primal value, a value so essential to its nature that if it were lost, the company would disappear with it. Next, the marketer must infuse the corporation-as-core-character with this value and put it into play as the protagonist's choices and actions build the story.

In practice, however, when corporations take on a core character role, the center often seems void. Some companies get the naming rights to a stadium in the hope of buying lovability. PR firms perform heart transplants by bedding their clients with charities. Philanthropy provides material for press releases, but its benefits seldom overcome the buying public's antipathy to multinationals. Always bear in mind that the center of good expresses itself in action, not association.

A corporate mission, however, tells another story. Starbucks, P&G, Royal DSM, and many other firms have taken up social causes such as educating the unfortunate, rebuilding after disasters, and curing third-world diseases. Not only do the stories these missions generate cast their corporations in a humanitarian role, thus drawing empathy, but—unlike self-congratulatory PR pieces—they also span a negative-to-positive arc that makes the purpose-told story a natural.

Brand Identification

Each person draws her personal identity from the culture that surrounds her. When asked who they are, people name their nationality, tribe, religion, profession, and marital status, along with the music, films, books, art, cuisine, and sports teams they love. They might add some experiences and achievements unique to themselves, but these, too, have been influenced by the culture that clothed them since birth. This was always the way of things until modern life added one more dimension: brands. In the first half of the twentieth century, people hid labels or cut them off. No longer.

Identification with brands, and the phenomenon of badging that came with it, arrived post–World War II and took up residence on Madison Avenue. Today people flaunt logos across their chests. These badges not only advertise the brand itself, but suggest their owner's taste, class, politics, sexuality, personality, and much, much more.

Brands, whether resource-, product-, or service-centric, are often more massive and complex than many third-world countries. They represent both a corporation in the background and a lifestyle in the foreground. Each brand radiates a presence in the world, surrounded by its own unique aura: IBM = genius, Budweiser = good times; Louis Vuitton = luxury. This essential quality has been earned through decades of hard work, so when a marketing story stars a corporation or its product, the brand's aura should become the protagonist's persona and the storytelling should reinforce this personality.[7]

Avoid Overdogs

When casting your protagonist, bear in mind the self-contradictory dynamics of your fellow human beings. A person can find her identity in anything from torn jeans to a diamond ring, from Big Macs to haute cuisine. So while people use products to shape their sense of self, that doesn't mean they empathize with the corporations that make them. People do not identify with power. They respect it, shelter in it, rebel against it, worship it, but they rarely empathize with it. The wealthiest of people, for example, often need high-end luxury goods to confirm their identity. Despite their obvious social prestige, they lie awake at night, feeling, in their heart of hearts, like an underdog. This perception is virtually universal.

When human beings survey their place in the world, they instinctively feel that they're up against overwhelming forces that stretch from the unpredictability of love to the inevitability of death. Weighed against the sum total of negative forces in life, we all feel, to some degree, on certain days, like an underdog.

When your story's inciting incident upsets the balance of your protagonist's life, the audience should sense that she is up against powerful antagonistic forces. The perception of underdogness draws empathy faster than any other cause. So above all else, avoid "overdog" protagonists. If you cast a corporation as protagonist, do not brag about its size, its reach, its wealth, its influence. If you cast a product as a protagonist, do not brag about its newness, its hipness, its celebrity. The world spares no empathy for an overdog; market with a graceful humility.

Step 3: Creation of Setting

Social and Physical Location

The social and physical settings for purpose-told stories range from the conceptual to the concrete, from animated to real-world grit, from a sole individual to a massive society. Compare the storytelling in two Apple commercials: "Get a Mac" and "Misunderstood."

The enormously successful "Get a Mac" campaign ran from 2006 through 2009 and told sixty-six different thirty-second stories. Each featured two characters symbolizing competing computer brands standing against an abstract, ultra-minimalist milk-white background. One dressed in casual clothes (actor Justin Long) and introduced himself as a Mac computer; the other dressed in a suit and tie (comedian John Hodgman) and declared that he was a PC. In each mini-story, a conflict quickly develops between the two "computers," then pivots around a single turning point, with the Mac always winning. The "Get a Mac" campaign received the Grand Effie Award in 2007.[8]

In "Misunderstood," realism rules as a true-to-life family celebrates Christmas in a true-to-life suburban home. The ad's ultra-naturalistic images tell the story of a teenage loner, surrounded by a lively family gathering, but spending his day face-deep in an iPhone. With a bolt of surprise, the turning point reveals that in fact the kid has used his iPhone to make a mini-film celebrating his family's joy-filled holiday. This ad played through the 2013 Christmas season and won a Creative Arts Emmy for Outstanding Commercial.

Wherever you physically and socially set the story defines and limits what's possible in the story. Only certain things are possible in a given world.

Location and Duration in Time

Now and then, advertisers set stories in the past, the future, or even the timeless worlds of the Brothers Grimm and Hans Christian Andersen to showcase everything from hair products ("Rapunzel") to bedroom furniture ("The Princess and the Pea"). But in most purpose-told stories, familiarity and accessibility guide the choice of temporal setting, placing the vast majority of these stories in a realistic, contemporary world.

Length of time is a different matter. Storytelling has the magical, piston-like power to compress time, turning an hour into an instant. A TV commercial, for example, might dramatize an entire wedding in thirty seconds, while an investment prospectus squeezes decades of corporate history into half a dozen pages. This works to a marketer's great advantage. You have the flexibility to use as much of the protagonist's life as you need to craft your story.

STAGE THREE: THE INCITING INCIDENT

An inciting incident launches a story by suddenly throwing its protagonist's life out of kilter, changing the core value's

Stage Three: Inciting Incident

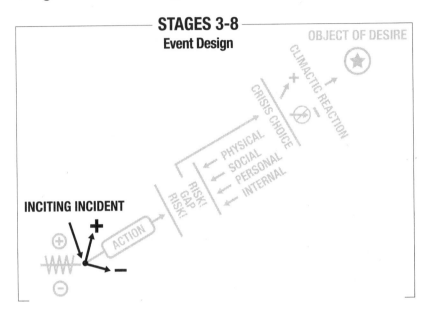

charge sharply to the positive or negative. This surprising event grabs the customer's curiosity and pulls him through the telling by raising a question only the climax can answer: "How will this turn out?"

In the purpose-told story, the precise quality of the inciting incident and the imbalance it causes depends on the nature of the protagonist. If, for example, your core character represents a corporation, possible inciting incidents range from mergers and acquisitions to takeovers and lawsuits. If your story stars a product, starting events run from innovation to obsolescence. If the consumer fills this role, anything can happen to a human being from giving birth to losing a loved one.

But no matter how you characterize your protagonist, his

reaction to the inciting incident should draw the audience's empathy and emotional concern, placing him at the story's center of good. By doubling involvement via both curiosity and empathy, you transform the customer's passing interest into suspense, laying the groundwork for the surprise that springs loose in Stage Five.

What's more, from the audience's viewpoint, the sudden reversal of fortune in the protagonist's life mirrors the customer's life and reflects his target need, the unsatisfied desire that the marketer discovered while researching the story's setups. This hook begins the mirror story that will carry the audience to climax and declare the call to action.

Consider, for example, the "December 21st" campaign created by Leo Burnett Madrid for Sociedad Estatal Loterías y Apuestas del Estado (SELAE), the Spanish national lottery.

As background, the Spanish Christmas lottery is the second oldest lottery in the world, operating continuously since 1812. Over two centuries, it has become a national phenomenon, with 75 percent of Spaniards participating in the annual drawing.[9] In 2016, the lottery sold more than €2.6 billion in tickets for its once-a-year Christmas drawing.[10]

The Christmas lottery operates differently from many other lotteries. There are just 100,000 potential winning numbers, from 00000 to 99999. The top prize (called El Gordo or "the Fat One" for this and other lotteries) pays €4M to each ticket holder who has selected the precise number drawn. In 2016, 165 winning El Gordo tickets won a combined €660 million.[11]

Individual lottery tickets cost €200, much more than most individuals are prepared to pay. Each ticket, however, is divided into ten perforated subtickets called *décimos*, enabling groups of people to purchase tickets together. Each *décimo* receives 10 percent of the winnings of each ticket. With this approach, the lottery unites friends and colleagues each year with a shared dream just before the holidays.

In recent years, social fragmentation in Spain has expanded beyond typical political debate, due in part to the growing Catalan independence movement. These divisions presented a threat to this shared ticketing model. Would groups form less often to buy tickets together? If so, would participating in the lottery be viewed as a selfish act? SELAE turned to storytelling not just to combat this risk, but also to position the lottery as something that helps unite people.

"December 21st" opens in a coastal Spanish town as a doting grandmother prepares a light breakfast of fruit, toast, and milk for her grandson. She thoughtfully arranges his meal on a tray and carries it to him in the living room.

The grandson, focused on his phone, absently dismisses her saying he is not hungry. As he does, the television in the room draws her attention, as an announcer calls the live drawing for El Gordo.

The grandmother rushes to find her ticket and watches in amazement as, ball after ball, her number is drawn. Stunned, she rushes out of the house to find one of the neighbors with whom she shared the winning ticket.

As soon as she departs, however, the television announcer returns, explaining, "And that's how the drawing went last year. Tomorrow is the big day."

Her son then enters, asking the distracted grandson, "Where's Grandma?" The grandson replies, "Outside to find [her friend], she thinks she's won the lottery." Suddenly concerned, her son starts after her, his life having been thrown out of balance.

The grandmother's misunderstanding triggers the inciting incident of the story. It hooks audience attention by causing viewers to wonder, "What will happen next?" That scene also establishes empathy for our protagonist. As the story progresses, the townspeople, SELAE's customers, emerge as a group protagonist. The worry on the face of one of the members of that group, her son, as he learns of her mistake draws the audience into empathy. As audience members, we realize that if our own grandmother were confused, thinking she'd found life-changing good luck, we would want to protect her from harm and find some way to cushion her from the fall, just as the son seeks to do by following her into the street.

STAGE FOUR: THE OBJECT OF DESIRE

Stage Four focuses the audience's curiosity and empathy toward the story's climax. In order to restore life's equilibrium, the protagonist conceives of the specific goal or objective, a story component we referred to previously as the object of desire. Like the inciting incident, the object of desire in a purpose-told story varies with the identity of the protagonist, be it an enterprise, product, or customer. This focus of intent could be a physical thing, like a new iPhone, or a condition that improves life, such as financial security, a career promotion, or even something more abstract like a dream of romance. To invent a one-of-a-kind telling, merge your knowledge with

Stage Four: Object of Desire

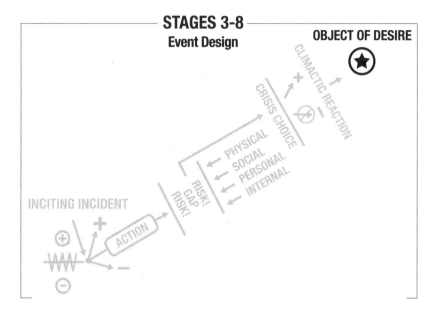

your imagination, and then ask: What exactly does my brand, corporation, product, or consumer want?

With that answer in hand, ask two questions more: How does this object of desire relate to the core value (for example, just/unjust or rich/poor) of the story? And by extension, how does the story's core value relate to my company's core value? Your answers need not match perfectly, but they cannot be divorced. Values and desires must reflect each other and thus unify the story with the company that produces it.

No matter how the object of desire is defined, as a thing or a situation, the central character feels he needs it to achieve a positive rebalance of his life. This desire drives him forward and powers your story.

In "December 21st," the town's object of desire is to help the grandmother avoid embarrassment and disappointment. To achieve that, a growing number of people will have to work together to execute an increasingly complex plan. As the story unfolds, the core value pair is revealed to be isolation/togetherness, taking us from the opening scene where the grandmother and grandson barely communicate to a very different conclusion.

STAGE FIVE: THE FIRST ACTION

Stage Five launches your protagonist's quest. To reach his object of desire, the core character takes an action based on his best sense of expectation. Spontaneously or consciously, he uses words and deeds as tactics to evoke the positive reactions

Stage Five: First Action

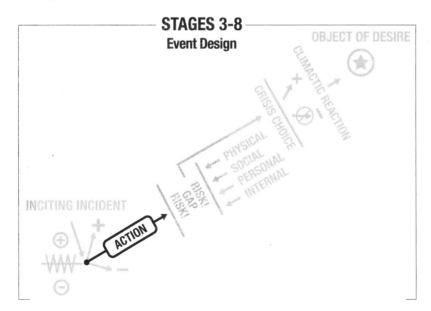

STAGES 3-8
Event Design

OBJECT OF DESIRE

CLIMACTIC REACTION

CRISIS CHOICE

PHYSICAL
SOCIAL
PERSONAL
INTERNAL

RISK!
GAP
RISK!

INCITING INCIDENT

ACTION

he hopes to get from his world. The unique identity of the protagonist determines the unique actions he will take.

Therefore, the creator of the purpose-told story must research the psychology of his core character in depth and detail. In the same way that the question "What would my character want?" demands knowledge and imagination, so do the answers to "What would my character expect to happen? And therefore what would he do to make it happen?"

Again if we turn to the "December 21st" example, the son takes the first action on behalf of the group protagonist when he carries the grandmother's jacket outside, expecting he will tell her and wrap it around her for comfort. Until...

STAGE SIX: THE FIRST REACTION

Stage Six violates the protagonist's expectations. A gap of surprise cracks open between what he imagined would happen when he took action and his world's sudden, unforeseeable reaction—a reaction that's either different or more powerful or both at once.

In the case of the Spanish lottery story, the son arrives to find his grandmother celebrating on the street with their neighbor, one of the other ticket holders who shares her number. The son and neighbor make eye contact, and the neighbor gives him a knowing look and shrugs, as if to say, *Let her have her moment.*

A full-length work of fiction may pull this reaction from any combination of the various levels of conflict (inner, personal, social, or physical). Most marketing stories, however, are compact and sharply focused on results. They therefore rarely involve their characters at more than one level of conflict.

Stage Six: First Reaction

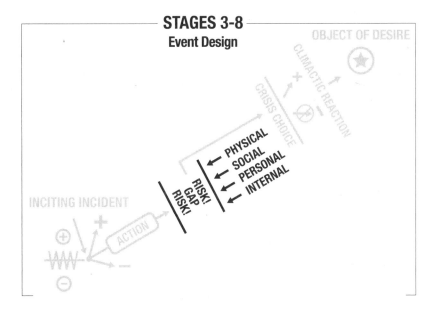

Developing a compelling story means developing a conflict that relates to your audience, mirroring the positive/negative duality of their lives. Think about it. Life fills our hours with problems to be solved, needs to be met, desires to be satisfied— not enough time to get the job done, too far to go to get what you need, a romance on the rocks, an illness that resists cure.

When negative forces block a character's desires, conflict compels her to reach deep within, make a tough choice, and then act. From the audience members' point of view, the protagonist's storied struggle mirrors their real-life struggle, thus focusing their attention, deepening involvement, and inspiring a purchase.

The creative force that rouses powerful storytelling is, as Jean-Paul Sartre taught, scarcity. There simply isn't enough of anything in this world to go around: not enough food, nor enough love, and never enough time. To satisfy human needs from their most basic to their most dream-filled, we must battle paucities that deny our yearnings. In short, the essence of reality is humanity's ongoing strivings against negation.

Imagine a TV commercial with three cheerful, homespun scenes strung back-to-back: a very happy family, followed by an even happier family, topped by the happiest family the world has ever seen.

What reaction would this triply sugared design evoke? The first spoonful might draw a smile, but the second will sour that grin, and the third will evoke a silent vow never to buy what's on offer. When mawkish ads drumbeat sentimentality, no one reaches for a credit card.

Marketing stories move from problem to solution, not solution to solution to solution. A positive climax demands a negative setup. For no matter how happy a happy ending may be, if nothing but uplifting scenes precede it, redundancy erases those images from the audience's memory.

The Law of Diminishing Returns

The more often a cause repeats, the less and less its effect.

Repetition kills impact. This principle, put into action, falls into a pattern of thirds, to wit: The first time we experience something it causes its full effect; the second experience causes half or less than half of its original effect; the third experience reverses itself and causes the opposite effect. The first piece of cheesecake tastes great; the second seems hard to swallow; the third makes you sick. The same pattern applies to story design.

Story enemy number one is repetition and leads to story enemy number two: vacuity. Why do so many branding campaigns devolve into boring recitations of... and then and then and then...? Why do so many product and service ads deliver little, if any, impact? Answer: because their tellings deliberately avoid any hint of conflict. And why is that? Answer: negaphobia.

Negaphobia: The Fear of All Things Negative

Negaphobia is a by-product of marketing education. Ever since the invention of the business school, and marketing as a unique discipline within its curriculum, marketers have been trained, as the old song goes, to accentuate the positive and eliminate the negative. What seemed like common sense and good manners has metastasized into an emotional contagion that now infects every dimension of corporate life from outbound branding to inbound team building. Today, for example, the worst thing one employee might say about another is: "He's so negative."

In all probability, the guy in question is simply a realist who sees things as they are, downsides and all, but from cubicle to cubicle, those who cannot face the sharp edges of reality tend to shun those who can. This negaphobic disdain for the truth is, of course, shortsighted, in that the career span of those who cannot face facts quickly abbreviates. So why would someone risk her or his future by ignoring what's real, no matter how negative? There are three primary causes:

First: as mentioned, the business school dictum to protect your brand from any and all criticism.

Second: the super-sensitive people of today's hyper-protective culture who find unpleasant truths intimidating.

Third: people who want to cover their asses.

Consider, for example, an ad with an intriguing negative

inciting incident that sets up a splendid positive flourish at climax, but, for some unknown reason, does not increase sales. The real cause for the ad's failure may be found in any link along the chain from creation to distribution, but the finger of blame will immediately point to whoever dared okay the ad's negative floor.

To preempt blame, marketing executives cover their butts by outlawing the least hint of anything negative in their ads. As an unfortunate result, negaphobia not only distorts their business judgment, but also sucks the impact out of their messaging.

The Principle of Negation

A compelling marketing story encompasses the negative of life. And the story must establish its negative floor either in Stage Two, when the inciting incident imbalances the protagonist's life, or here in Stage Six as the story's forces of antagonism suddenly react against the protagonist.

This surprise instantly pops the question "Why?" into the mind of character and audience alike. Curiosity drives them to look more deeply into the story's society and setting. As they suddenly discover the answer, they experience a rush of insight into the true forces that oppose the protagonist's desire and how his world actually works. Consumers love to realize the truth in this spontaneous, storified way. They want to be shown, not told. They don't want to sit in a classroom; they want a surprising living discovery.

This insight puts the consumer's mirror story on a path to solution and the satisfaction of her need. She doesn't know how it will be done, but it's out there, so she can't look away. This curiosity holds your prospect's attention, even in a world of constant distraction.

Marketing stories are generally brief. The protagonist pursues her object of desire through usually only one turning point.

However, in longer stories, such as our "December 21st" example, stages 5 and 6 build progressively.

Progressive Complications

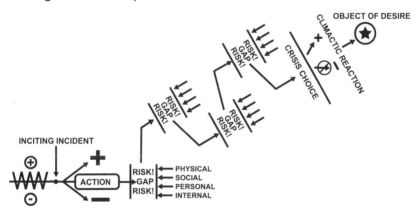

The antagonistic force that violated the protagonist's expectations in Stage Six now blocks the path to her object of desire. At the same time, however, this unforeseen reaction gives her a new understanding of her world. In Stage Seven, she puts this insight to work as she makes her final choice of action.

STAGE SEVEN: CRISIS CHOICE

Stage Seven brings the story to its crisis, the highest level of tension and suspense. The protagonist, based on her new knowledge, chooses a new tactic, one she hopes will create a reaction from her world that will deliver her object of desire.

Stage Seven: Crisis Choice

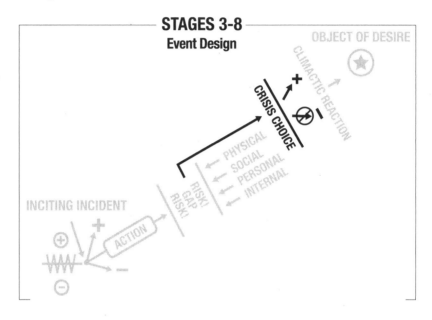

At this point in most fiction-told stories, the protagonist stands in dilemma, forced to choose between either two irreconcilable positive possibilities or two equally repugnant negative choices.

Never in a marketing story. Rather, the insight the protagonist gained in Stage Six now gives her a clear choice of what to do to get what she wants. She conceives her new tactic and takes it.

As the protagonist acts, tension peaks and the audience senses that the world's next reaction will answer the major dramatic question: "How will this turn out?"

Events progress in "December 21st," until the protagonists realize the day is coming to a close. As a wonderful lobster feast winds down, they know the grandmother will soon learn there is no €4 million prize coming her way. Her son makes the decision that they must tell her, and approaches to break the news.

Stage Eight: Climactic Reaction

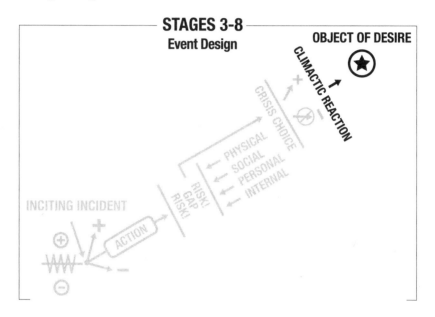

STAGE EIGHT: CLIMACTIC REACTION

Stage Eight delivers the goods. The protagonist's second action evokes a positive reaction from his world, giving him his object of desire and reestablishing the balance of his life. This climactic event not only satisfies your audience's emotional curiosity about the outcome of the story, but also dramatizes how they can solve the mirror problem in their own lives—how they, too, can get what they need and desire.

Early in "December 21st," after the son's first attempt to protect his mother fails, he and the neighbor, Puri, agree to celebrate her "win" at the pub. Immediately forces of antagonism arise. The pub owner and other guests know the lottery drawing has not yet happened. A single word from one passerby will shatter her extraordinary day. As the grandmother walks across town, her family and friends call ahead to alert the pub owner and ensure everyone there is ready to play along. Champagne is being poured as they arrive.

After celebrating in the pub, the grandmother sets off to greet friends at her salon. The town involves more people to keep up the ruse, and a crowd begins to grow behind her.

At one point, she wonders, "Shouldn't the television crews have arrived?" Her son nearly throws in the towel and reveals the truth, but he's stopped by the previously disinterested grandson. Caught up in the spirit of the day, he sprints off to find friends with a video camera who can interview Grandma. While the townspeople thought that might satisfy her, at the end of the interview she turns to the crowd and marshals them to the town lighthouse for a town-wide celebration.

"December 21st" ends with a final twist. Before the son can break the truth to the grandmother, she stops him, saying, "I know what you are going to say." He sighs, thinking she has already figured it out and been let down. Instead she reaches into her pocket and hands him her "winning" lottery ticket, saying, "But you should always listen to your mother. And I will be much happier if you have this."

He hugs her, makes eye contact with Puri, and they decide to let the ruse go on. In that moment, the audience is rewarded with a rush of insight. It was not the windfall of money that made the grandmother so excited. It was the happiness that she knew it would bring the town, in the many ways they might celebrate and live better together. We realize as the screen fades to black that, through their adventure that day, they had achieved that happiness through togetherness, whether El Gordo winners or not. "December 21st" executes its progressive complications brilliantly, holding the audience's attention to climax.

The Open-Mind Moment

A story's climax impacts the audience's mind with a sudden rush of meaningful emotional insight, a flash of "I get it!" In this instant, a flood of charged understanding opens the mind. Neuroscientists have measured this open-mind phenomenon and found that it lasts for six to eight seconds. In this moment of wonder and pleasure, anything presented to the mind lodges in its memory. Therefore, this is the spot where the wise marketer plants his logo. That's exactly what the Spanish lottery does at the end of their five-minute story, and beneath it they feature their tagline "There's no bigger prize than sharing."

The Call to Action

The final effect of the open-mind moment turns the entire story into a massive *call to action* that sends the audience member out into the real world to duplicate the protagonist's triumph. Wanting to relive the mirror story, she purchases the product or hires the service that's at the heart of the story.

EXPLICIT VERSUS IMPLICIT STORYTELLING

Now that we have reviewed the eight stages of story, it's important to note that not every marketing story needs to take its audience through all eight stages explicitly. The mind, as we noted, is a story-taking and -making machine. One key phrase or image may imply an entire story, as the audience's mind instantly imagines the unexpressed stages.

Consider, for example, Nike's famous imperative: "Just Do It." What story do those three words imply? It goes like this:

"I'm climbing the stairs one day and barely make it to the top [protagonist in his setting]. I suddenly realize that I've got to get in shape [inciting incident] before the stairs kill me [object of desire: fitness]. I buy a pair of Nikes and start to run [first action]. The pain hits hard [first reaction]. But I stick with it [second action]. Each day I push against the pain until I lose weight, feel great, enter the local 10K [second reaction/climax].

"Call to action: Buy Nike."

A story doesn't even need words. Take for example, the famous Michelin advertisement, featuring this image:

What story runs through the mind at the sight of that ad? It might go like this:

"I'm driving [consumer as protagonist] along a curvy road on a stormy night, my family in the backseat [setting in balance]. Suddenly a truck jackknifes in front of me [inciting incident], putting them at risk [object of desire: a safe, secure family]. I swerve to the side [first action], my tires splash into the mud [first reaction]. But as I swing around the spinning truck [second action], my Michelins grip the shoulder and I veer safely past the truck, and back onto the asphalt [second reaction/climax]. Thanks to my Michelins, I save my family's life.

"Call to action: Buy Michelins."

When told beautifully, a little goes a long way.

PUTTING STORY TO WORK

Introduction

Compelling subject matter promises a story worth telling, and mastery of story craft fulfills that promise, but to transform how your organization connects with its customers, the telling must be skillfully aimed and purposely told. And for that process to work, it needs a champion. This section begins with a look at the role the CMO plays in this new story-driven world.

Once your organization has mastered story form, you must then learn to craft different types of stories to achieve different objectives. Part 3 explores the application of story to achieve four key goals: branding, advertising (to extend the life span of the current model), demand and/or lead generation in a post-advertising world, and sales. Once we have examined story application, we will examine how to measure the impact of your storytelling against the specific goals you set for it.

7

STORY AND THE CMO

As brand storytelling rewrites modern marketing, what role will the CMO play? In a recent interview, GE's CMO Linda Boff discussed the seismic shift happening in marketing.[1] When we asked what future role the CMO will play when this transformation is complete, Boff replied:

> You'll have to pardon me on this one, because I just watched *Steve Jobs* over the weekend with Michael Fassbender... and there's a line in there where Steve Wozniak says to Steve Jobs, "You're not an engineer, you're not a product guy, you're not a programmer. What the hell do you do?" And Jobs says, "I conduct the orchestra."
>
> Well, I'm no Steve Jobs... but I also think the two essential roles of the marketer are conducting the corporate orchestra and setting the North Star vision...

The primary focus of the lead marketer has been advertising campaign creation and optimization. CMOs polished the plans of their predecessors, made adjustments to include new outlets and technologies, and boosted performance over time. Today the CMO occupies a new, critical, and far broader role in the company than ever before: change agent.

THE CMO AS CHANGE AGENT

Patterns of information and entertainment consumption have shifted so radically that every enterprise must adapt across every function. Companies that update their customer-building techniques will achieve market leadership; those that don't will fade away as their competitors, born to this new ecosystem and engineered for its success, replace them. Today's CMOs must adapt her entire enterprise to a new reality.

Your first task as change agent is to educate your executive team on the worldwide shift from ad-centric to story-centric marketing. No small task. Conventional C-suite wisdom holds that six-year-olds crave stories, while hard-charging executives don't. But you know that if your company doesn't change its MO, it won't survive, so you must build a winning case to convince the C-suite.

First, draw on the scientific research covered in chapter 3 and demonstrate how story fits the mind. Explain how this fit provides an unparalleled opportunity to connect the minds in your company with the thoughts and feelings of your customers. Next, to win your case, master the techniques found in chapter 13 and then prove how the positive impact of storytelling can be measured and geared to success.

Once your executives are on board with the concept, teach the eight stages of story creation to sales, marketing, product development, communications, investor relations, and leadership at all corporate levels. Finally, to put storytelling into practice, coach your team to change their thinking habits in six decisive ways:

1. Change your team's analytical method from deductive logic to causal logic.

With unparalleled access to big data, executives often assume that given a sufficiently broad set of consistent observations, they can infer a general truth about the world. But business leaders who use induction as their sole basis for understanding the world often miss the causal links necessary for insightful decision making.

Suppose, for example, a diaper company were to commission a big data study that showed only a minuscule percentage of people born in 2010 use diapers, while virtually 100 percent of those born in 2017 wear them. If the marketing team were to stop thinking beyond these numbers (in other words, if they were to ignore the toilet training that causes them), they might happily forecast skyrocketing diaper use among the young and ramp up production.

As absurd as this hypothetical may seem, the pattern is, in fact, commonplace. For decades now, number-based inductive logic has blinded many executives to causes and effects. Results can be ruinous. Coach your team to search below the surface of data for the hows and whys hidden in those depths.

2. Change the team's sales practices from additive to progressive.

Your education trained you to tell the world the good and only the good about your company. Facing a willing listener, you list as many positive attributes as possible—"My company does this and this and this and this and this and this and this"—until you've exhausted the poor guy. In truth, you lost him with your first brag because a sophisticated client knows that there's good and bad in everything. If you present nothing but the good, he knows you're hiding the bad. He considers that lying and decides you cannot be trusted.

In a storied approach, you progress by dramatizing an initial value change to begin the telling, then build to a greater value change, and climax on the greatest value change, revealing both the successes and obstacles along the way. Your story's progressive complications hold the attention of your audience while sharing a more complete, trustworthy, and convincing version of what you do.

3. Change the team's worldview from narrow and shallow to wide and deep.

How does a story create meaningful value change? Through conflict. As outlined earlier, life contains four levels of conflict: physical (battling a hurricane, a disease, the ticking clock of time), social (struggles against institutions, perhaps discrimination, red tape, or power plays), personal (antagonisms inside intimate relationships) and inner (wars within the mind over conflicting desires).

Dove's "Real Beauty" stories drive their campaign by foregrounding the inner conflict of self-criticism versus self-appreciation. Apple's 2013 iPhone Christmas commercial pivoted around a misunderstanding within a family. Always's #LikeAGirl stories draw on the social antagonisms that cause systemic low self-esteem among women. In the last chapter, we discussed how the Michelin baby-in-a-tire ad used life-threatening conflict on the highway to tell that company's story.

Train your teams to work through all levels of antagonism so they can craft stories that resonate with the consumer.

4. Change your team's understanding of values.

Convincing storytelling depends on an authenticity of values. Therefore, a transformational CMO ensures that the company has a strong core value that resonates with the entire team, that drives decision making inside the organization, and, ultimately, that inspires brand storytelling.

Your stories should be entertaining, but they cannot be mere entertainment. They serve a greater purpose. By representing the core values of your business in the stories you tell, you have the opportunity to influence how people feel about your brand and increase their likelihood of purchase. We'll explore how to accomplish these goals in chapters 8, 9, and 10.

5. Change your team's marketing theory to embrace emotional intelligence.

Marketers often begin their work by asking, "What facts do my customers need to know about my company's products and services?" They then design their campaigns to convey those particulars.

But the trouble with the fact-driven technique is this: The key to decision making is emotion, and emotion is not information. The emotionally targeted question you should ask is: "How do I want my customers to feel?"

Your team members must frame their stories to create a feeling of fusion between protagonist and audience. When empathy seals the deal, use progressive conflict and value charge changes to hook and hold your audience, and finally reward it with a story climax that reinforces brand or product values.

6. Change the team's mental model from static description to dynamic storytelling.

Take away PowerPoint platforms and teach team members how to convert data to drama.

THE CMO AS SHOWRUNNER

I want to be a showrunner.

—Linda Boff, CMO of GE

We do not suggest that the CMO create her brand's stories personally. Rather, we would cast the CMO as a showrunner. *Showrunner* is the showbiz title for the master creator/producer behind today's brilliant long-form television series. This is the keeper of the vision, she who projects the story's arcs, season after season, and at the same time ensures that every detail in every scene not only harmonizes with the whole but also sets up future payoffs.

As corporate showrunner, the modern CMO educates her team in story craft, produces a storytelling strategy for the brand, and operationalizes its storytelling processes. She recruits the right creatives, guides moment-by-moment storytelling to ensure brand/voice alignment, and exercises good taste to guarantee a quality experience for the brand's prospective customers.

It's a big job.

8

STORIFIED BRANDING

Every CMO starts his day staring at this hard truth: *Nobody wants to hear about your company or your product.*

For more than two centuries, marketers weathered this resistance by interrupting the ongoing pleasures of captive audiences with advertising. Some fortunate brands today triumph over advertising by reaching the saturation point of public awareness. When Apple or Samsung brings out a new gizmo, news media make it front-page stuff and die-hard fans line up without seeing an ad. Those rarities aside, people do not spend their day waiting to hear about a new style of jeans or hip flavor of yogurt. Typically, consumers only debate brands in the mental minute just before they make a purchase. That precious minute makes storified branding an imperative for modern marketing.

The chapters ahead reveal how the purpose-told story incites a call to customer action, but this chapter first examines how branding stories lay the foundation for that action by cementing the brand in the consumer's mind and surrounding that image with positive associations. Brands that seal this emotional bond—GE, IBM, Always—succeed; those that don't, struggle.

Let's begin with a look at what *brand* means in the twenty-first century.

DEFINING BRAND

Patrick Davis, CEO of Davis Brand Capital (DBC), developed a method for analyzing markets and developing differentiated brands. Marketing leaders such as Anheuser-Busch, InBev, Autotrader, Chipotle, Progressive, Target, and Verizon attest to the excellence of Davis's system. All rely on DBC to help fathom, design, and develop corporate and product/service brands.

In a recent interview, Davis laid out his vision of the modern brand:

> Brand is a single organizing idea, a higher-order construct that everything else comes from and aligns with. Sometimes I liken it to the fresh water that makes everything else possible, whether that is growing your crops or cleaning your clothes or making soup. It's that ingredient that goes across everything else.
>
> Finding a fresh source of water that won't be depleted and can be used in hundreds and hundreds of ways is a challenge. Which is to say [brand] is intangible, it is abstract, and it is true. It has to be all of those things at once.
>
> The job of the marketer is to make it tangible and real and to work with its truth to tell a story that is compelling whether it happens in one image or three lines or

a long-form piece. All of that is in service of saying we want brands to be a link between a number of positive associations for the consumer, and increasingly for communities and constituencies beyond the consumer, to say that we can all come together around this one big higher-order idea.

It is a belief system, and like any belief system, it has its language, it has symbols, it has rituals, and behaviors to go with them.[1]

One clear example of brand rituals weaving through our culture is the phenomenon of badging.

Davis explained: "What it means to hold a Bud Light is very different from what it means to hold a Budweiser, which is very different from what it means to hold a Stella Artois. Those brands are all owned by the same company, and in fact, consumers may choose those brands at different points in their weekend, because they are conveying different aspects of their personality with that badge, with the beer bottle they are holding." The brands we choose reflect how we see ourselves or, perhaps, how we want the world to see us.

Originally, Davis pointed out, brands were simply a means of identifying the producer. The purpose of the brand was to show that a certain person had made that specific piece. Whether silver goods or porcelain or leather goods, wares were hallmarked by their maker (in effect, they were branded like cattle). Through that brand, the maker was taking responsibility for the quality of the goods. If the buyer had a problem, she could return to the maker for satisfaction. Today, however, Davis notes, "The mark is just a shortcut, a signal for [the brand]. [The brand] still exists and survives beyond the product and beyond the mark and that's when you get into some very interesting work."

How can you create a brand that matters so much to people that they make it part of their self-expression? For generations, television advertising did the trick. Not anymore. To connect with audiences today, we need a different approach. And it had better be good, because we've got a steep hill to climb.

THE MODERN ANTIPATHY TO CORPORATIONS

On September 18, 2015, the United States Environmental Protection Agency (EPA) accused Volkswagen of knowingly and willfully violating federal law by selling 428,000 diesel cars equipped with "defeat devices." Volkswagen programmed these cars with special software designed to evade environmental tests. When tested in a lab, their diesel engines operated more efficiently (but far less powerfully), meeting required environmental standards. When later operating on the road, they operated differently, emitting nitrous oxide at forty times the legal limit.[2] Prior to this announcement, the company compounded its problems by providing a series of false justifications to the EPA, in attempts to explain why environmental road tests did not match lab results for the diesel vehicles they sold from 2008 through 2015.

Volkswagen's CEO resigned five days after the EPA announcement, claiming he had no knowledge of his team's decision to intentionally evade environmental standards.[3] When lawsuits related to the scandal were finally settled, the number of affected cars had climbed to 580,000. Volkswagen paid $20 billion for its crimes.[4]

In addition to environmental damage, Volkswagen customers suffered direct harm: Nobody wanted their used cars. In the resulting settlement, the court ruled that customers were eligible to receive thousands of dollars back on their previous car purchases to make up for lost resale value. But to many of these customers, who bought their fuel-efficient Volkswagens because of their personal commitment to the environment, no rebate could compensate for Volkswagen's breach of trust.

Five years before, on the morning of April 20, 2010, an explosion rocked the *Deepwater Horizon*, a mobile, offshore drilling unit that was drilling a deep-water well for BP in the Gulf of Mexico. Eleven of the 126 members of the crew on board were killed in the fireball. The fire could not be extinguished before the *Deepwater Horizon* sank to the ocean floor, five thousand feet below, thirty-six hours later.

The explosion and resulting spill created the worst environmental disaster in American history.[5] The US government summarized the recovery effort, reporting:

Oil flowed from the well for 87 days. Two drilling ships, numerous containment vessels, and a flotilla of support vessels were deployed to control the source of the well, while 835 skimmers and approximately 9000 vessels were involved in the cleanup. On the single most demanding day of the response, over 6000 vessels, 82 helicopters and 20 fixed wing aircraft and over 47,849 personnel/responders were assigned; 88,522 square miles of fisheries were closed; 168 visibly oiled wildlife were collected; 3,795,985 feet of containment boom was deployed; 26 controlled in situ burns were conducted, burning 59,550 barrels of oil; 181 miles of shoreline were heavily oiled; 68,530 gallons (1632 barrels) of dispersant were applied, and 27,097 barrels of oil were recovered.

An estimated 4.9 million barrels of oil spilled into the ocean during the disaster.[6]

US District Judge Carl Barbier found that "BP's negligent acts that caused the blowout, explosion and oil spill...were profit-driven decisions." He concluded, "These instances of negligence, taken together, evidence an extreme deviation from the standard of care and a conscious disregard of known risks."[7] BP and three BP employees were also charged criminally. The company pleaded guilty to eleven felony counts of misconduct or negligence for the deaths resulting from the initial explosion.[8] After facing more than one hundred thousand lawsuits from businesses and individuals affected by the spill, BP estimated in July 2016 that the disaster cost the company $62 billion.[9]

These aren't just any companies. Volkswagen is the largest automaker in the world.[10] BP is the sixth largest oil and gas producer in the world.[11] Just two years earlier, banks around the world were accused of risky lending practices that nearly crashed the global economy.

The willingness of these companies to put profits above the well-being of their customers, their neighbors, and the environment has not just damaged their individual reputations. It has damaged the perception of businesses in general.

The Edelman Trust Barometer found that just 52 percent of

people living in democracies worldwide trust corporations, and that trust is eroding. What's more, they believe the problem begins at the top: Just 37 percent of those surveyed find CEOs to be credible.[12]

Years of abuse have left people disenchanted with corporations and skeptical of their claims. On a far broader scale, the bragging and promising that have defined modern advertising have eroded trust further. Most everyone knows that products on offer probably won't give them fewer wrinkles, whiter teeth, a slimmer waistline, or a happier marriage, as promised again and again. Sick of being fooled, people assume that the phrase *for profit* means "at any cost," even the possibility of harm to the consumer.

Overcoming skepticism is like overcoming gravity. It's a natural force, buttressed by the endless bragging and over-promising of brands.

STORY AND THE PSYCHOLOGY OF INFLUENCE

The well-told story erases skepticism by wrapping the story's meaning inside an emotion. The source of this psychological power is empathic identification. Once an audience instinctively links its sense of self with a protagonist, doubt vanishes. The protagonist's choices and actions become the audience's vicarious choices and actions. Each change in value charge in the protagonist's life sends the audience through the same emotional twists and turns. When the core character's final action wins her object of desire, emotion and meaning fuse—without a word of explanation.

Like an epiphany, a story's climactic action floods the mind with a sense of truth. Because the audience member's own thoughts spontaneously form this idea, she believes in it without rationalization or any hint of skepticism. It's hers, after all. What's more, the pleasure-filled emotion aroused by this sudden insight engraves the experience into her memory. From that day on, her upbeat remembrance surrounds the brand with a subliminal halo that influences her purchases. This is how stories, consistently told well, establish a meaningful brand in the minds of consumers.

THE SEARCH FOR SUBJECT MATTER

Once you determine your audience (Stage One of the storytelling process), you must choose subject matter that contains a physical and social setting, a core value, and a protagonist (Stage Two). Subject matter possibilities for brands fall into at least five grand genres: origin, history, mission, product, and customer stories. You need a least one story to define your brand, but some brands tell thousands.

Origin Stories

In the comics, origin stories explain how a superhero achieved his uncanny powers and driving desire for justice. A radioactive spider bite infused Peter Parker with amazing arachnidan skills, but it wasn't until a thief murdered his uncle—a murder he could have prevented if he had used his superpowers—that Peter took on his secret crime-fighting persona known as

Spider-Man. This origin story not only dramatizes how Spider-Man became Spider-Man, but also uses the humanizing combination of guilt, courage, and humility to build a lasting empathy for this bizarre character.

For companies known for innovation, successful branding often begins with a founder-as-protagonist origin story. Apple's, for instance, began in 1976 when Steve Jobs and Steve Wozniak were bit by the urge to create a home computer in their garage. Corporate wisdom at the time claimed that the only buyers for these machines were businesses with complex needs, but that view was obviously wrong, and today's Silicon Valley tells an anthology of origin stories based on the landmark garages where businesses like Apple, Google, and HP were born.

Once again, empathy. Genius-in-a-garage stories are as old as Thomas Edison. They touch the heart because they star the iconic American business hero: a young shoestring entrepreneur battling shortsighted prejudice and overwhelming odds. If your company has a powerful origin story, and the core value of that story aligns with your brand's, make it the first story you tell to establish your brand in the minds of your consumers.

Corporate History

In truth, however, successful businesses rarely begin with action movie heroism. They take root in three things: a good idea, hard work, and persistence. Denied a compelling origin, corporations often try to build brand affinity around a chronology of events that would only interest the C-suites and board. Too often these tellings become bland narratives listing positive events in the corporation's history. As we pointed out in chapter 4, stories progress with emotional dynamics; narratives repeat emotionless facts.

Consider, for example, the Coca-Cola website piece titled "125 Years of Sharing Happiness."[13] It makes a grand promise . . .

> This is the remarkable story about the evolution of an iconic brand and the company that bears its name. Since its birth at a soda fountain in downtown Atlanta, Georgia, in 1886, Coca-Cola has been a catalyst for social interaction and inspired innovation. These unique moments in history, arranged in chronological sequence, have helped create a global brand that provides billions of moments of refreshment every day.

. . . that it does not keep.

Would this chronology hook the attention of Coke's typical customer? Hold her interest? Pay it off? Make her feel anything? Coke marketers asked that emotion-killing question: "What do we want our customers to know about Coke?"

During the 2017 Super Bowl, Coke reran "It's Beautiful," an ad taken from the 2014 Super Bowl, reaffirming its corporate commitment to cultural diversity—a positive position but still not told in story form. Throughout its marketing history, Coke has been content with soft narratives (their home page in January 2016 featured articles including "A Food Historian's Take . . ."), anti-stories (recipes, instructions, where-to-find-it maps), and a bottle shaped like the *Venus de Milo*.

Coke owes its first hundred years of global dominance to twentieth-century advertising. For this iconic brand to maintain

1891

Calendars are first used for advertising by Asa Candler. Note the ad for De-Lec-Ta-Lave, a mouthwash that is also sold by Candler. After 1892, he focuses his energies exclusively on Coca-Cola.

1892

Asa Candler, who began to acquire The Coca-Cola Company in 1888, finalizes the purchase and incorporates The Coca-Cola Company as a Georgia Corporation.

An advertising budget of $11,000 is authorized.

1893

The Coca-Cola Spencerian script trademark is registered with the U.S. Patent office.

At the Company's second annual meeting, the first dividend is paid to investors.

1895

Asa Candler declares in the Annual Report that Coca-Cola is sold and drunk in every state and territory in the United States.

1890s

or even increase its 40 percent market share, it will have to do what twenty-first-century beverages like Red Bull have already done—go story.

Mission Stories

If your founding story lacks against-the-odds excitement, if your corporate history marches through time with professional but boring progress, your company can still find empathy-enhancing stories by taking on a mission. *Mission*, in our definition, means a service to humanity that goes beyond writing a check to a well-known charity.

Millennial and Generation Z consumers want, indeed demand, public service from private enterprise. They believe profit comes with a social responsibility to make the world a better place. Naive or not, it's what the under-forty market expects. In response, many corporations, big and small, have taken up missions. The most famous mission (and inspiration for many that followed) is Starbucks's Corporate Social Responsibility Initiative (CSR).

Three like-minded examples:

1. Procter & Gamble

Ever since Hurricane Katrina in September 2005, when a disaster, natural or human-made, strikes anywhere in the United States, Tide's Loads of Hope program ships truckloads of washers and dryers to families in the midst of chaos. Tide's executives know that clean clothing helps to put desperate people back on their feet.

2. Royal DSM

This Dutch multinational specializes in nutritional and biomedical products, so it naturally partners with the World Food Program, but DSM also supports small teams of scientists working to solve global environmental and health problems. Watch DSM's mission-focused storified video *Unsung Heroes of Science*.[14]

3. Costa Del Mar

This French-owned, Florida-based manufacturer produces high-quality polarizing sunglasses, using biodegradable materials. CDM's Kick Plastic campaign strives to reduce the Texas-size plastic garbage patches swirling in the world's oceans.

These missions generate story after story that star either the corporation as the protagonist or a surrogate who labors in its stead. Both roles are immediately empathetic because, given the way of things, anyone who tries to do good in this world is automatically an underdog. Marketers at mission-driven companies should strongly consider telling stories that align with their respective missions on their websites and in their advertising.

Product Stories

Apple followed its origin story with a brilliant product story, a massive metaphor first told for the 1984 Super Bowl. In Apple's iconic commercial, an athletic young woman symbolizes the Macintosh computer, and her revolt, in turn, symbolizes the Mac revolution.

Clad in bright red shorts, storm troopers at her heels, she runs through an otherwise gray world and down the center aisle of a cinema. On screen, a propaganda film celebrates the anniversary of the "information purification directives," the words echoing over a submissive audience, hypnotized by the promise that the oppressive, dominant technology will prevail.

The ad cleverly linked the ubiquitous IBM business computers to the Orwellian society from the novel 1984, in which all decisions were controlled from on high. In the climax of the ad, the woman hurls a Mjölnir-inspired hammer toward a giant screen. The propaganda images shatter, liberating the audience by destroying the symbol of the state. She risks all to achieve the object of her desire, and as we celebrate her success, the narrator explains: "On January 24, Apple Computer will introduce Macintosh. And you'll see why 1984 won't be like 1984." It was a powerful statement, one that resonated deeply with an

America in the midst of the Cold War, facing the Soviet Union's totalitarian regime.

The same core value of rebellion versus submission resonates in Apple's trademark. It's not an apple, Patrick Davis pointed out, it's an apple with a bite taken out of it. That image retells the foundational story of Judeo-Christian heritage. The first bite from the tree of knowledge celebrates humankind's greatest act of rebellion.

Apple's branding stories, with their product-as-protagonist and mythical trademark, dramatize the company's core values of liberty over compliance, creative thinking over rote thought.

Consumer Stories

If none of the four story sources above work for your enterprise, where do you turn? To the ultimate source—the consumer.

The success case most frequently cited is Red Bull's. This company doesn't have an origin, history, mission, or product worth talking about, and yet it found an ingenious way to build its brand.

Red Bull's market researchers first discovered that their die-hard customer is a young guy who loves extreme sports. Digging deeper, the executives asked, "What do our customers want to feel?" The answer came back: "Frenetic energy." This insight led to their discovery of the brand's core value: excitement/boredom. The next logical step was to tell online consumer-centric stories that couple powerful writing with original pulse-pounding film to dynamically dramatize the company's core value from the consumer's point of view.

One such tale, for example, follows a mountain biker, Claudio Caluori, as he wheels across the sharp edge of a mountain peak in

Virgin, Utah. The path he follows appears to be just a foot wide in spots. The mountain suddenly drops away thousands of feet on either side. You, in empathy, react to his risk; your heart beats faster. A treacherous spot looms ahead, and Claudio faces a critical decision: hop over a gap in the track and shave critical seconds off his time or take a safer, slower route. With a leap, Claudio risks his life and a rush of white-knuckled excitement runs through us, followed by relief as he lands on solid ground. In that open-mind moment, the Red Bull brand appears on screen connecting its image with the charge you just felt. That's branding through story.

This is why when you visit Red Bull's website, you won't find a picture of a Red Bull can or any bragging about its contents. Why? Because Red Bull recognizes that its typical fifteen- to twenty-five-year-old male customer doesn't care about what's in an energy drink. In fact, he doesn't even think about energy drinks except the moment he walks into a convenience store and opens the fridge. The marketers know that if a guy who's watched RedBull.tv sees a choice between Red Bull and a competitor, he will recall the edge-of-his-seat emotion their storytelling pocketed in his mind and reach for their brand—without fail.

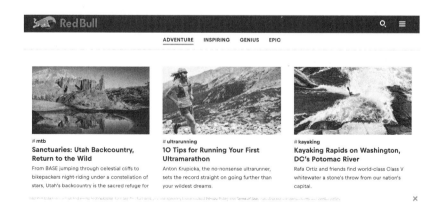

Red Bull, as in the examples above, tells male-centered stories at the level of physical conflict. Procter & Gamble, in sharp contrast, gears its female-focused stories at the levels of inner and social conflict. Consider, for example, the P&G product Always and its #LikeAGirl branding campaign.[15]

Once again, research. The Always team at the Leo Burnett Agency discovered that the sneering insults "You run like a girl" and "You throw like a girl" demean not only women in general, but the Always target audience in particular—pubescent girls. "Like a girl" undermines self-esteem at a critical time when profound hormonal changes in a girl's body go to war with her sense of self, body and soul struggling to forge a new identity.

The only cure to inner pain is perceptual change. And in this case, it began at the cultural level. Always created a video that does not mention feminine hygiene, Always products, or the ways they might be better than the competition. Instead it takes all-girls-everywhere as a massive, empathetic group protagonist, and in one powerful turning point tells the story of their struggle to overcome this taunt. At climax, empowered girls reverse the phrase's connotation from negative to positive until #LikeAGirl becomes a symbol of female strength.

The Internet audience shared their pride and linked that feeling to the Always logo. As of this writing, the #LikeAGirl video had been viewed on YouTube more than one hundred million times in 150 countries.

After its initial online success, Always turned the #LikeAGirl campaign into a 2015 Super Bowl ad. Adobe reported that #LikeAGirl drove more engagement than any other ad that year. Four hundred thousand people shared the ad with tens of millions of followers on social media during the game; 84 percent of those mentions were "extremely positive."[16]

#LikeAGirl became an Internet meme, with successful women adopting the hashtag used by Always to encourage the next generation. Always may have launched the campaign, but it was the public that took it to the next level, turning Always into a more meaningful brand.

THE MEANINGFUL BRAND

Havas Media defines *meaningful brands* as those that inspire the thought, *This brand improves my life.* This sense of enhancement envelops both the consumer and the brand in an aura of well-being.

In America, we often mistakenly equate happiness with financial success. While the two are correlated, a person's sense of well-being versus ill-being depends on the moral emotions moved by the values of right/wrong, fair/unfair, loyalty/betrayal, and justice/injustice at play in his life. A poor person, for example, can live in a state of well-being if he looks back at his days and feels that the world has treated him justly and his poverty, therefore, is due to his own choices, his own actions. A wealthy person, on the other hand, may suffer in misery if he feels that, despite his best choices and actions, an unjust world has cheated him. The former finds life meaningful; the latter questions it.

The *World Happiness Report*[17] reveals this to be the rule, not the exception. The *Report* analyzes global data to identify whether and to what extent macro aspects of life, such as economic growth/employment, political stability, and democratic form of government, or micro aspects, such as individual income, personal freedoms, marital relationships, and social support networks, affect happiness.

The *World Happiness Report 2017* offers this perspective on America today:

> The central paradox of the modern American economy, as identified by Richard Easterlin (2016), is this: income per person has increased roughly three times since 1960, but measured happiness has not risen. The situation has gotten worse in recent years: per capita GDP is still rising, but happiness is now actually falling.
>
> The predominant discourse in the United States is aimed at raising economic growth, with the goal of restoring the American Dream and the happiness that is supposed to accompany it. But the data shows conclusively that this is the wrong approach. The United States can and should raise happiness by addressing America's multi-faceted social crises—rising inequality, corruption, isolation, and distrust—rather than focusing exclusively or even mainly on economic growth, especially since the concrete proposals along these lines would exacerbate rather than ameliorate the deepening social crisis.[18]

Put simply, we want more from life than money. People want genuine human connection, to be treated fairly, and to be treated honestly.

Given this context, to create a meaningful brand in the minds of consumers, it must be authentic. Consumers find a brand trustworthy and meaningful when two stories match:

the story the brand tells about itself and the story the public tells about the brand. Therefore, regardless of the story you choose to tell, all brand stories must follow one simple principle: The core value of the story must match the core value of the brand. If these stories do not align, if promises made are not kept, the public feels betrayed and their sense of injustice indicts the brand as detrimental to their lives.

In the past, this double-edged phenomenon was known as word of mouth. Advertisers bragged and lured consumers with guarantees; consumers tried their product/service; stories followed, told to friends and family, that either confirmed or denied the brand's boasts.

Today, thanks to the Internet, word of mouth is instantaneous and ubiquitous. Consumers constantly judge and grade every product/service of every brand on a scale of 1 to 5, followed by a story told to the world, dramatizing, for better or worse, the consumer's experience.

Meaningful brands use the various modes of storytelling listed in this chapter to explicitly and/or implicitly dramatize their promises. When a product/service's story matches or even exceeds the consumer's hopes, "word of net" propels a *This brand improves my life* message viral and imbues the brand with a humanized meaning.

Havas reports that meaningfulness drives disproportionate financial results. Their global study of a thousand companies, employing three hundred thousand people, in thirty-four countries, across twelve industries, found that fully meaningful brands "... see their marketing KPIs perform 100 percent better overall compared with less Meaningful Brands."

In fact, every 10 percent improvement in "meaningfulness"

increases purchase intent by 6.6 percent, repurchase intent by 3.2 percent, customer advocacy by 4.8 percent, and premium pricing by 10.4 percent. Meaningful brands gain, on average, 46 percent more share of wallet than those ranked as not meaningful. What's more, meaningful brands outperformed the overall stock market by 133 percent.

The facts are clear: Marketers whose brand stories match consumers' stories see their tales retold as consumer identification drives significantly better returns for team members and shareholders.

9

STORIFIED ADVERTISING

Man, I am so glad I saw that advertisement.

—Nobody, ever

GE had a problem. Chairman and CEO Jeff Immelt had successfully led GE's transformation from a company with a very large financial services business into what leadership now calls a "digital industrial company." The company had shifted gears to capitalize on a more connected world, where massive linked machines provided opportunities for new, sustained revenue streams, much the way the consumer-focused Internet of Things has begun to do in our personal lives. Today GE's portfolio is focused on transportation (aviation and rail), health care, and energy. But just making the machines was insufficient. The company would need the best engineers, thousands of them, to fully realize Immelt's vision.

"One of the things that we have made a big bet on," explained Linda Boff, CMO,[1] "is the digitization of industry. We are now living in a time when simply selling the hardware, if you want to call a jet engine a piece of hardware, isn't enough. We need to be in the business of helping our customers gain productive outcomes. And to get to results, we have created a whole group, thousands of people, primarily new to the company, that have a deep software background. [They] are building the analytics and data that will enable our customers, whether it's a rail customer or aviation or a power plant or a food and beverage corporation, to operate more effectively, more cheaply, or more productively by being able to anticipate where there are efficiencies... that might be being able to predict whether a jet engine needs to come off-plane to be maintained... or where a wind farm needs to expand next."

But before they could recruit the world's most talented engineers who would write the new software to run, monitor, and optimize the performance of the planes, trains, and wind farms, GE needed to get the word out about its new direction. Most software engineers didn't realize that GE had begun tackling complex, interesting challenges in technology, and those engineers were still flocking to jobs at the FANG companies (Facebook, Amazon, Netflix, and Google), as well as Apple and Microsoft.[2]

GE's marketing team was tasked with changing how engineers viewed the company. Boff started with a story. She said: "I believe, and our team believes, that idea-generated media is going to win out over programmatic, no matter the scale. We are buyers of impact, not frequency. Partly because we can't spend enough to achieve frequency, and partly because I really do believe that ideas break through." So her team worked with GE's agency to create a story.

Enter Owen.

GE's protagonist Owen is a young graduate engineer

who got a job with GE. The campaign "What's the Matter with Owen?" captures how Owen's friends and family react to the news. In one spot, his parents, excited that he'll be working at GE, give him his grandfather's sledgehammer. Owen has to explain that he won't be building machines, he'll be writing the code that lets them talk with one another. In another, he shares news of his new job with a group of friends at a picnic table. Another friend announces that he has just taken a job at a fictional company called "Zazzies."[3] Zazzies offers an app where you put fruit hats on pictures of animals. His friends are big Zazzie fans and are thrilled and distracted by the second announcement. "I'll be helping turbines power cities," Owen protests. "I just put a turban on a cat," his friend counters. "I can make hospitals run more efficiently," Owen offers. "It's not a competition," a friend chimes in.

The ads delivered powerful results. Not only has Owen helped bring GE's brand into alignment with its new strategy and portfolio, but the campaign has increased job applications from software engineers tenfold. All thanks to a good story.

When you storify advertising, you build an emotional connection between your brand and your audience. Owen is an underdog. We all imagine ourselves to be underdogs in the world. We identify with Owen when he is misunderstood by the world. We empathize with him and, by the end of the story, we want the world to understand that Owen is doing something important. He is creating software that makes big machines work far better than ever before.

Now imagine if GE's ads said that directly: As the company logo fills the TV screen, a voice intones, "We at GE create the software that connects the biggest and best machines of this world." Would audiences believe it? Or care? Doubtful. The Owen stories touch emotions bragging could never reach. That's power.

PUT A STORY WITHIN THE STORY

Although the long-term future of broadcast advertising seems bleak, television and radio will remain marketing platforms for those who can afford them for some time to come. So if your strategy calls for disrupting dramas and comedies with ads, then do it as tactfully as possible by putting a story within the story.

The mind jumps from story to story rather easily. For example, when viewers change channels in search of something good, or when story lines crosscut from central plot to subplot and back, audience engagement switches gears in a heartbeat. Story always feels welcome. So when your ad interrupts one story with another, the transition seems relatively smooth, but when you break deep, ongoing narrative involvement with a bragging/promising sales pitch, people hate it and ignore it.

Consider the Super Bowl of commercials, the Super Bowl. This is the only day of the year when you'll hear that odd rebuke, "Quiet, guys! It's the commercials!" For a good reason. Brands and their agencies work all year to craft stories to fill most of these ad spots.

Super Bowl fans argue about their favorite ads during the game and then publish best and worst lists online the next day. Have you ever noticed that old-school bragging/promising ads tend to sit at the bottom of those lists, whereas storified ads rush to the top?

Storified ads win off the field as well. When brands do their homework and truly come to understand their customers, they can craft stories that disrupt markets.

In India, for example, marketers for the laundry detergent brand Ariel found deep disparity in the social norms for women and men in the household. Seventy percent of men believed their wives should do the laundry. Even among children, two in three believed women were responsible for household chores.[4] Today women in India spend an average of six hours each day on housework, compared with men who spend less than one.[5] While this difference itself is unfair, it contributes to far broader inequality over time.

Young women have nearly two thousand fewer hours a year to study and prepare themselves for careers, leading to fewer and lower-quality jobs and depressed wages. Women who are already in the workforce have less opportunity to advance because they must balance work and home life differently.

The share of India's workforce comprising women fell from 31 percent to 24 percent between 2004 and 2011. Declining workforce participation has an adverse effect on the lives of women and the overall success of the Indian economy, as Harvard professor Rohini Pande has explained: "Working, and the control of assets it allows, lowers rates of domestic violence and increases women's decision-making in the household. And an economy where all the most able citizens can enter the labor force is more efficient and grows faster."[6]

Indian women long for change. Eighty-five percent of Indian women reported feeling like they have two jobs, one at work and one at home. Eighty-three percent believed men should share the burden of household work.[7] Marketers at Ariel and their agency BBDO India (Mumbai) understood this growing inequity and tapped into its social undercurrent, a growing sense of injustice, with their ad "Share the Load."[8]

"Share the Load" opens with the voice of its protagonist, a grandfather, narrating a letter that he writes to his daughter while she races around her home one evening. As he watches her juggle work, making tea for her husband, and caring for her children, the grandfather becomes increasingly aware of how he passed these social stereotypes on to the daughter he raised.

The story establishes a powerful negative floor by demonstrating how these norms have passed and continue to pass from generation to generation. Then the story turns from negative to positive when the daughter reads his note and discovers the grandfather's promise to share the burden of housework with his own wife and model the way for others.

The shift in the core value pair at stake here, from injustice to justice, connected with Indian women and ignited a conversation across the country. The *Share the Load* video was viewed more than fifty million times in fifty days. It generated more than 2 billion earned impressions online, the equivalent of $11 million in ad spending had that exposure been purchased. Talk shows devoted entire episodes to discussing how to balance the role of men and women in the household. Major clothing brands changed washing instructions on clothing tags, adding "May be washed by men or women" to traditional instructions. More than two million men visited the Ariel website (a laundry detergent site) and signed a pledge to #ShareTheLoad. Dating sites then added a new question to profiles, "Will you share the load?" This allowed people committed to finding a better balance to find one another.[9]

The social impact of this storified campaign must have delighted marketers at Ariel almost as much as this statistic: Sales of Ariel in India grew 75 percent year over year.[10]

Storified commercials are far more engaging and effective than those that brag and promise, but in a world where consumers seek uninterrupted experiences, they will never be sufficient. With millions of consumers shifting to ad-free experiences every month, marketers must adjust their approach as well.[11]

The modern marketer must offer her customers unique, valued, and, most important, fluid, nonstop experiences. In the same way that media companies built and maintained their audiences for decades, brands, too, must tell stories at a sustained pace to earn the respect of their customers and keep it.

10

STORIFIED DEMAND AND LEAD GENERATION

The average tenure of a chief marketing officer is just forty-four months.[1] To survive, CMOs need to demonstrate that they can deliver business results quickly. Many senior marketers arrive on the job to find they do not have time to invest in branding. Their company needs demand generation (B2C) or lead generation (B2B) to achieve quarterly results.

Historically, in tight quarters CMOs would ramp up the advertising budget to meet revenue goals, or cut the budget to meet earnings. But with the rapid decline of advertising reach and efficacy, they need to turn somewhere new. To understand how brands can drive consumers to purchase and business buyers to engage with sales teams, we need to consider how people discover and consume information and entertainment today.

Throughout the twentieth century, people got their daily news from some combination of the morning paper, drive-time radio, and evening television. Today fewer than 27 percent of

Americans can name a single top-ranked newscaster or print journalist.[2] Instead online searches drive their active discovery, while social media provides for passive discovery.

ACTIVE VERSUS PASSIVE DISCOVERY

To gain immediate knowledge, people today turn to Internet search engines like Google, Bing, Yandex (Russia), and Baidu (China), as well as voice searches like Apple's Siri, Microsoft's Cortana, Google's "Hey Google" (on Android and Google Home), and Amazon's Alexa. More than 175 billion times per month, someone somewhere launches one of these goal-driven, active discoveries.

Over the same four weeks, thirty billion people with no specific goal follow curiosity where it leads to Facebook, Twitter, LinkedIn, Instagram, Snapchat, or Pinterest, and by pure coincidence learn something interesting, something of value. These chance revelations often feel like a gift from beyond, so people share their passive discoveries with friends and family, compounding these serendipities from thirty to ninety billion.

These tens of billions of discoveries offer an unprecedented marketing opportunity, if you provide the information or entertainment your customers seek.

Analysts who study online consumer behavior report that 85 percent of the time, when people click away from a search page, they click not on a tab or an ad, but on a link to something else. When they click away from social media, that number jumps to 90 percent.

This means that like blank billboards along a highway,

search and social discoveries offer CMOs new ways to reach customers and build ongoing relationships, but if marketers fill this space with ads alone, they will miss the vast majority of their addressable market. The solution, therefore, is to reach customers through sustained content creation, rather than the hit-and-miss of traditional advertising.

What's more, when someone arrives on your website, what's the first thing he sees? Your products? Your logo? Your slogan? A list of claims? Really? Never underestimate the power of first impressions. When your customer first arrives, consider giving him a gift.

CONTENT MARKETING

Content marketing creates material your customers want or need, instead of repeating messages describing the features and benefits of your company or products.

Content marketing is not new. In 1895, John Deere launched *The Furrow*, a magazine that helped farmers work more skillfully and profitably. *The Furrow* still exists and reaches 1.5 million readers in more than forty countries. Explicitly, it provides the innovative techniques farmers need; implicitly, it builds awareness of John Deere farm machinery.

In 1900, a French manufacturer launched a guide to fine restaurants, hotels, and sightseeing destinations. The publication executed its mission with such consistent excellence that it became the journal of record in that space. Today one of the highest honors awarded any restaurateur is a "Michelin Star." Not bad for a tire company.

As *The Furrow* and the *Michelin Guide* demonstrate, the strategy of content marketing has been, since its inception, simplicity itself: *First, give them a gift.*

Before the sales pitches begin, before claims and guarantees assault the buyer, put a hand out and in it place a gift of meaningful, emotional experience. Welcome the client with an insight she's never had before, wrapped in a feeling she's never felt quite that way before. In short, tell her a story.

If a visitor's first impression of your brand is a captivating video or a fascinating piece of writing that tells a story rooted in nature, science, history, or some other new and interesting subject matter, this surprise gift opens the door to your store. Now she's inside, looking around, and your visitor moves from anonymous consumer to prospect. Let your sales team take her the next step from prospect to customer.

In the past, content marketing projects, such as *The Furrow* and *Michelin Guide*, were a costly way to supplement advertising. Brands had to identify prospective audiences, research and author up-to-date subject matter every week or month, print that content, package it, and pay distribution fees. Today, no. Brands like Colgate with their Oral Care Center[3] or IBM with SecurityIntelligence.com provide always-on experiences that improve the lives of their prospective customers.

The globally connected world makes publishing and distribution tasks relatively simple and their costs nominal when compared with the costs of printing, marketing, and delivery of traditional media. Moreover, when marketers engineer content for easy discovery in search and social, earned reach hits unprecedented scale. Skillful execution of sustained storified content marketing minimizes audience-building costs, and thus drives far greater ROI than interrupt advertising.

As a result, brand marketers who have never played the content marketing game now rush onto the field. For CMOs new to the sport, however, understanding the options and ascertaining which work best for a particular business can be rather confusing. To address this problem, and guide marketers through the steps they must take to move from ad-centric to story-centric marketing, we have created a framework called the Marketing Continuum.[4]

THE MARKETING CONTINUUM

This continuum spans the five developmental stages of companies incorporating content marketing into their strategies. Are you a bystander, creating only product-focused content? Or a leader working to storify your marketing and sales? Using this framework, you can diagnose where your organization sits today and guide your step-by-step transformation from ad-centric to story-centric.

Content Marketing Continuum

The Bystander

Bystanders are addicted to the past. These companies get a high from continually applauding themselves, bragging about their products, and promising the moon. Like all addicts, they can't see that other people do not share in their self-indulgence. So the CMO of a bystander company must, like a therapist, transform the thinking of the executive, marketing, and sales teams, and then lead them to focus on the needs and desires of their customers, not themselves.

The Novice

Novice brands take the first step and publish customer-centric content, but, compared with their more evolved competitors, novices remain novices because they're strung out on the age-old strategies of advertising campaigns—they publish sporadically in short time frames but then, sensing the weakness of this tactic, spend most of their marketing dollar to buy audience from the media outlets they hire to create and publish their content.

For example, sometimes novices purchase space from media companies to post one-off info-ads designed to help prospective customers master a skill that is related to their offering. The content helps the customer solve a problem while demonstrating that the brand can be a helpful adviser.

Vanguard offers a retirement planning column and calculator to educate prospective customers about why they should contribute to their IRA accounts at the start of the tax year instead of at the end. Canon helps camera owners find innovative ways to

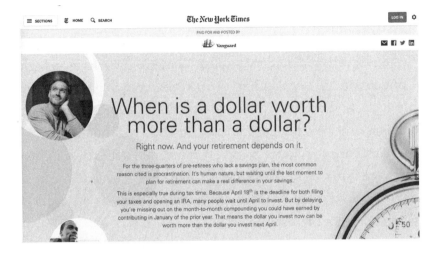

exercise their craft by sponsoring interviews with famous photographers about inspiration.

At the *New York Times*, in fact, you can buy a native ad package with an internal team called T Brand Studios that will help you develop your info-ad and a promotion scheme to drive *New York Times* subscribers to it.

Social platforms saw this opportunity coming years ago. When the various social media first launched, they sold ad space for revenue but let companies freely publish content to anyone they wished. For a while, these brands enjoyed vast social reach as their material was consumed, commented on, and passed

along to friends. Before long, however, social platforms changed their algorithms and eliminated this organic audience.[5]

All short-term, campaign-based solutions, by definition, lack a regular publishing rhythm, so there's no incentive for the consumer to return. For that reason alone, campaign-driven content strategies will not drive meaningful results. They offer the novice easy ways to test the waters, but no more than that.

The Expert

Experts do not rely on one-off or campaign-based habits. Instead they give their customers sustained, dependable experiences that educate, inspire, and entertain over time. The Oral Care Center, for example, is Colgate's gift to its customers.[6]

In this section of Colgate.com, current and prospective customers find helpful information on how to keep their teeth and gums healthy, as well as tips for dealing with more difficult dental procedures like extractions and implants. People seeking solutions to dental problems click on Colgate far more than the traditional medical sites of WebMD and the Mayo Clinic.

How did Colgate.com become the most trusted source for dental info? First, the Oral Care Center team finds the topics customers search most and then creates content to match. They ensure each article is optimized to rank well against search queries.[7] By search optimizing content, Colgate.com creates an experience that ends the search. Customers find what they need. Every month Colgate.com broadens its audience and builds relationships that last.

Second, Colgate does not use the Oral Care Center to promote the benefits of Colgate products. Brands lose credibility when

Google | how many teeth do we have | 🔍

All   Images   Shopping   News   Books   More   Settings   Tools

About 121,000,000 results (0.93 seconds)

32 teeth

At about age six most children begin to lose their baby teeth, which are then replaced with adult teeth. This process will continue into their early teens. Adults have more teeth than children; most adults have **32 teeth**. Among these teeth are 8 incisors, 4 canines, 8 premolars, and 12 molars (including **4** wisdom teeth).

How Many Teeth Do We Have | Colgate® Oral Care
www.colgate.com/en/us/oc/oral-health/...teeth.../how-many-teeth-do-we-have-0113

❓ About this result   ▦ Feedback

People also ask

How many baby teeth do you have?   ⌄
How many teeth do you have at the top of your mouth?   ⌄
How many teeth do you have when your 3 years old?   ⌄
How many different types of teeth do humans have?   ⌄

Feedback

How Many Teeth Do We Have | Colgate® Oral Care
www.colgate.com/en/us/oc/oral-health/...teeth.../how-many-teeth-do-we-have-0113 ▾
At about age six most children begin to lose their baby teeth, which are then replaced with adult teeth. This process will continue into their early teens. Adults have more teeth than children; most adults have **32 teeth**. Among these teeth are 8 incisors, 4 canines, 8 premolars, and 12 molars (including **4** wisdom teeth).

they shift the focus of their content from helping the customer back to the bragging and promising of yesteryear.

Instead the Oral Care Center content positions Colgate as a leader in oral health and delivers clear benefits to prospective customers. This shift from creating content about the brand to creating content that the customer actually seeks makes Colgate a content marketing expert.

The Leader

Companies evolve into content marketing leaders when they move from sustained content creation to sustained storytelling.

Four years ago, IBM unified its security products and services inside one division: IBM Security. Today IBM Security employs eight thousand security professionals, adding nineteen hundred since 2015. IBM's $2 billion security business grew by double digits, twice the rate of the market, in 2016.

Caleb Barlow, VP IBM Security, explained their unique marketing challenge: "What we have is a very technical issue, a very complex issue, and in some cases a very scary issue that we need to be able to describe to people in order to get them to act. We're not talking about products, like a collaboration system, that you log in to and use all day every day. We're talking about products that, hopefully, you never see as an end user, and in some cases hopefully you never need to use. But boy, you'd better make sure they're there when you need them. So storytelling becomes extraordinarily important."[8]

Leaders at IBM Security realized that chief information security officers and the general public have two very different needs. "The popular media, when we are talking about a cyber breach," Barlow said, "focuses on whodunit and why they did it...If you are the next potential target, you care about how it occurred— not why, not whodunit, but how? Because if we focus on the how, then we actually have the opportunity to solve the problem."

IBM Security realized that the company could develop an audience of CISOs, CEOs, and board members concerned with security by creating a journal of record focused on the "how" in the IT security space. The resulting property, IBM's award-winning SecurityIntelligence.com, breaks news on hacks, malware, data theft, and software vulnerabilities that can put enterprises at risk, and analyzes how others can avoid the same attacks.[9] Hundreds of thousands of CISOs, CIOs, and CTOs visit and return to that property each month and are grateful to IBM for the help.

How is this different from advertising? Why would consumers trust this information from IBM, but distrust advertising from brands? Caleb Barlow knows that a company loses credibility when it brags about itself or makes promises about its products. So the vast majority of the content on SecurityIntelligence .com does not mention IBM, its products, or its solutions. Instead IBM simply provides the information that IT professionals need to do their job. As a result, some believe IBM's credibility on IT security ranks higher than any traditional news source.

When IBM uncovered a hacking threat to petrochemical plants, it aired those threats on SecurityIntelligence.com. The world listened.

After the article appeared on the site, traditional news orga-

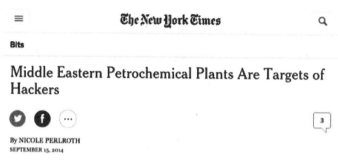

Middle Eastern Petrochemical Plants Are Targets of Hackers

By NICOLE PERLROTH
SEPTEMBER 15, 2014

SAN FRANCISCO — Security researchers at IBM said they had uncovered a series of hacking attacks aimed at Middle Eastern petrochemical companies.

The researchers, at IBM's Trusteer division, said the hackers were using a variant of financial malware known as Citadel, which was first discovered in 2012.

Citadel was originally engineered to steal victims' banking credentials by capturing their keystrokes and taking computer screenshots. But the researchers said that hackers targeting petrochemical companies have altered Citadel to add more functions: to take complete control over a victim's PC and allow hackers to gain access to a victim's corporate network. They have also made modifications in the

nizations like the *New York Times*, the *Wall Street Journal*, the Associated Press, and Thomson Reuters all relayed the story around the world, linking it to IBM SecurityIntelligence.

"If you're buying a security product, it's kind of like buying a child seat for your kid: You're not interested in second best," Barlow explained. "It's practical, but it's also emotional."

When C-suite executives decide it's time to make new investments to keep their company safe, their first call goes to IBM Security because the brand became their trusted adviser through the stories shared on SecurityIntelligence.com.[10] This is the secret all content marketing leaders know very well.

Driving Demand with Story

In chapter 8, we learned that stories told for the purpose of branding must observe one important rule: The core value of the story must align with the core value of the brand. The setting for these stories, such as surfing the big wave, could be unrelated to the product being sold, such as an energy drink, so long as the core value aligns with the brand promise. In Red Bull's case, both take you from fatigued to energized. But until Red Bull bet big on story-centric marketing, there was no link between their brand and the extreme sports they now cover each day.

When we apply story form to demand/lead generation marketing, however, we apply the same form differently. In demand/lead generation stories, the protagonist will typically be a customer or prospective customer. The inciting incident will occur, at least in part, because the protagonist is not using the product/service your company offers. This will take the customer to the negative. When an object of desire forms in the protagonist's mind, your offering is one that will help her achieve that goal.

Demand/lead gen stories will typically end on the positive, with the protagonist achieving her object of desire, in part with the help of an offering like yours. In a handful of cases, however, like Adobe's famous "Click Baby Click" advertisement,[11] the story ends to the negative, with implied disaster for the protagonist. "Click Baby Click" opens in the headquarters of a sleepy encyclopedia company. The inciting incident is a spike in web traffic and orders, driving sales through the roof. News climbs quickly to the CEO, who proclaims, "We're back!" and then marshals the resources of his suppliers around the world to quickly ramp up production. Commodity markets for wood pulp skyrocket, responding to sudden demand for more paper. But the segment ends with the revelation that the driver for this demand wasn't a rebounding marketplace, hungry for encyclopedias; it was a single small child who liked pushing the BUY button on an iPad. As the scene fades to black, the audience knows the featured company and CEO protagonist face certain economic disaster. But then, after the story ends, Adobe takes us to the positive with a message to the audience: "Do you know what your marketing is doing? We can help." In effect this final reveal shows that your fate doesn't have to be that of the CEO, if you are smart enough to buy the Adobe Marketing Cloud to analyze your data.

To use a story that ends on the negative effectively, marketers turn to comedy, as does Adobe. In comedy, the cardinal rule is that nobody actually gets hurt. If you do not employ comedy, you risk creating negative feelings about your brand—like Nationwide did when they ruined the Super Bowl for millions with their infamous commercial "Boy" in 2014. The spot featured an empathetic young protagonist that the brand killed in a bathtub.[12] The day after the spot aired, *USA Today* covered how the audience reacted on Twitter to this misapplication of story form.[13]

The Nationwide example illustrates that story form, applied improperly, can do damage to your company just as effectively as story well told and well applied can do good.

Create? License? Curate?

When a CMO launches a sustained content marketing regime, where will she get her stories? Will she create originals? License them from other sources? Or simply curate stories others created?

Original, sustainable story-driven content creation is not

easy. Marketers with this ambition must develop a strategy, license a content marketing platform (CMP), recruit creatives, and implement a process for managing, reviewing, and improving that content every day. A regular publishing cadence of well-told stories requires time, money, and resources.

For that reason, some marketers cut corners and try to license or curate instead. Licensing content means that they pay a fee to media companies for the rights to pre-written stories or pre-produced videos. Curation eliminates fees by simply citing media stories and sending audiences to the original source.

Although content licensing and curating are cheap and fast, both are inherently flawed. If you use either means, how can you differentiate yourself from your competitors? What's to stop your competition from emulating you, using the same content from the same sources? And most important, if you curate or license, how do you demonstrate thought leadership and expertise the way IBM Security does?

Jeanniey Mullen is Global CMO of Mercer, a firm that provides advice and technology-driven solutions to help companies meet the health, wealth, and career needs of a changing workforce. Mullen taps Mercer's health, wealth, and career thought leaders to craft the stories that drive their marketing. In a recent interview, Mullen explained, "Technology is radically reshaping how we work and how we interact with our colleagues. With over 21,000 employees in offices in 140 countries, we're on the front lines with our clients, studying that change and defining how companies adapt to and capitalize on it. We *are* the experts. We have to be, that's our business. There is nowhere else to get this information and our clients must have it to compete and succeed."[14]

In their recently-launched effort Mercer Digital,[15] Mullen and her team share what they discover about the changing marketplace. For example, she explains, "Today there is intense competition for talent. Millennials are looking for different things from a job than their older counterparts. [Millennials] know how quickly the world is changing, so they care much more about ongoing education and new skills development than Gen Xers did when they entered the workforce. Companies can't just present traditional benefits packages to this generation; they need to show them how they will prepare them for career mobility in the future.

"Alternatively, in fields with increasing automation, we're now helping companies prepare their workforce for 'cobots' or collaborative robots. How do you orient someone to work hand-in-hand with a machine? What can they expect? How do they interact? What are the safety requirements? What additional training is required? How can the machines be designed for better human interaction?" By gathering this insight from Mercer experts around the globe and sharing it on Mercer Digital, Mullen uses original content to demonstrate the firm's unique expertise while simultaneously creating value for customers and prospects alike.

At the same time, Mullen sees another benefit from original content creation over licensed. When a brand licenses or curates from various sources, it loses its voice. Every media company you might license content from writes in its own voice, from its own perspective, speaking with its own tone. "What we write has to be quintessentially Mercer," she explained. "If it's not, we aren't building a relationship with our customer."

To succeed, tell original stories regularly and consistently in your own voice. Do this and do it well and you, too, will become a leader in content marketing. Shortcuts won't work.

Think Big

The five traditional sources for marketing subject matter (origins, histories, missions, products, consumers) provide a wealth of material—but within certain constraints of time and quantity.

If a CMO has a vision beyond those limits, where could he go to generate content marketing on a massive, international scale over decades?

In 1975, Britain's Peninsular and Oriental Steam Navigation Company (P&O), then the world's largest shipping company, partnered with executive producer Aaron Spelling to provide its ship, the *Pacific Princess*, as a setting for Spelling's new television series titled *The Love Boat*. Every week for more than ten years, audiences watched an attractive set of guests board the *Pacific Princess* and sail in near-perfect weather to stunning destinations where they fell in love (or back in love), all within an hour. *The Love Boat* became a top-five prime-time show that was dubbed or subtitled in dozens of languages and remains in syndication to this day.

As Princess Cruises president Jan Swartz told the news website *Mashable*, "I think before the TV show, virtually no one had heard of the idea of taking a vacation at sea on a ship . . . So what the show did was introduce into the living rooms of American families this concept of a wonderful ocean-going escape."[16]

The show's writers did not sell P&O's vacation line, they simply created romantic comedies that linked feelings of love and fun with the Princess Cruises brand. When the series began, just five hundred thousand Americans took a cruise each year. Today more than twenty million set sail. Thanks to *The Love Boat*, Princess Cruises went from a fleet of just two ships in 1975 to eighteen today, multiplying the company's gross annual income 9000 percent.[17]

Should a company today create its own television series? Or thinking even bigger, should a company purchase an entire sport or broadcast rights to a league?

Every sporting event tells a living story. Each contest rolls out a dynamic tale of winning/losing, from the inciting incident (the first pitch/first tee shot/the kickoff) to the climax (the last out/the last putt/00:00 on the clock). What's more, sports spin off unlimited ancillary stories about the players, coaches, officials, owners, and leagues.

Would it make sense for a mega-company like Coca-Cola, Mastercard, Anheuser-Busch InBev, or GM to purchase the rights to a sports team, a league of teams, or even an international championship, and then use those games and their subsidiary subject matter to generate material for its content marketing?

On May 17, 2014, the *New York Times* reported that NBC-Universal had licensed the broadcast rights for the six Olympic Games spanning the years between 2022 and 2032. NBC paid $7.75 billion and secured not just the television rights, but what the *Times* described as "exclusive rights to broadcast the Games on whatever technology emerges between now and then."

The price tag for the deal made headlines, but NBC paid it, confident that the investment would drive value because sporting events are one of the last bastions of the traditional broadcast advertising model. "As more viewers consume media on their own schedules, often without commercials," the *Times* reported, "broadcasters regard live events as the only content that compels most viewers to watch in real time, as one vast audience, without filtering out advertisers."

The broadcast ad model still performs during sporting events, but does that mean major brands should cede this territory to media companies and their aging ad models? Did mega-brands miss an opportunity when they failed to bid against NBC?

Let's do the math. Coca-Cola spends approximately $4 billion in annual global marketing.[18] Over the eleven years from 2022 through 2032, that would amount to $44 billion. The NBC bid came to about 17 percent of that. Acquiring the rights to broadcast the Olympics in North America, and then share its stories with the world, would have been a high-rolling bet for Coke, consuming a major chunk of its total marketing spend.

On the other hand, every two years, the world would turn to Coke, and Coke alone, for the Olympics stories people love—all the stories that build up to the games, the month-long games themselves, and then the limitless spin-offs. By simply swapping the Coca-Cola logo for the NBC Peacock, the company would have created a differentiated experience that connects its products with the joy the Games bring.

Well over $600 billion was spent on interrupt advertising last year. Mega-corporations will need to decide whether buying broadcast rights to events like the Olympics or World Cup or Super Bowl might make sense one day. They'll need to decide whether producing their versions of *The Love Boat* might build a lasting, meaningful connection with their audience.

But one thing is certain: As the broadcast ad model rapidly declines, sharing great, original real-life or fictional stories will become the only way mega-brands can differentiate in a consumer-driven world. And there's money to it. Out of the hundreds of advertising billions spent each year, many leading companies could easily afford to transform themselves into international storytellers.

Smaller companies with tighter budgets have no choice; they cannot afford to spend precious capital on advertising that yields less each year. Their future hinges on their mastery of the storytelling craft.

The Visionary

A few years after he founded Amazon, Jeff Bezos sensed that his executive team members had lost their edge—their ideas seemed dull and clichéd, their thought processes flabby and shallow. He had to know why, so he dug in, researched, and unearthed a surprising but clear cause: His C-suite heads were simply forgetting how to think.

Amazon executives were having so much fun designing PowerPoint slides, they never bothered to figure out how things actually worked, how one thing caused another. They just glossed over ideas, flattened out priorities, and ignored the interconnectedness of forces within Amazon itself, as well as among Amazon, the market, technology, and both national and international politics. Bezos needed wide-ranging complex minds, in-depth thinking, executives with broad, long-term insight. So in June 2004 he sent his Senior Team (S-team) the following memo:

```
From: Bezos, Jeff
Sent: Wednesday, June 09, 2004 6:02PM
To: [REDACTED]
Subject: Re: No PowerPoint presentations from
now on at S-team
A little more to help with the question "why."
Well-structured, narrative text is what we're
after rather than just text. If someone builds a
list of bullet points in Word, that would be just
as bad as PowerPoint.
    The reason writing a good six-page storied
memo is harder than "writing" a 20 page Power-
```

```
Point is because narrative structure forces bet-
ter thought and better understanding of what's
more important than what, and how things are
related.
```

As Bezos later told Charlie Rose: "The traditional corporate meeting starts with a presentation. Somebody gets up with a PowerPoint display, some type of slide show. In our view you get very little information, you get bullet points. This is easy for the presenter, but difficult for the audience. And so instead, our meetings are structured around six-page narratives. When you have to write your ideas out in complete sentences, complete paragraphs, and tell a complete story, it forces a deeper clarity."

To think in story form, Bezos told Rose, means hard work. His executives have to imagine all the interconnecting forces that affect Amazon's enterprise—from bottom to top, from past to future, from personal to global. So to prepare for an Amazon meeting, S-team members must first create, then write out, print out, and pass out a six-page story. For the next twenty minutes or more, the team reads these stories in silence around the table during what Bezos calls "study hall."

Bezos instituted this practice because he wants his people to think first and foremost in the causal logic of story structure, both vertically and horizontally. *Vertically* meaning thinking in depth and asking, "What are the true, deep, invisible causes of what's happening now?" *Horizontally* meaning thinking through time and asking, "What past events made this happen and what will be the future consequences of these previously hidden causes?"

Aristotle advised the enterprise leaders of Athens to "Think like a wise man, but speak like a common man." Harvard Business School paraphrases the adage into "Think with complexity; speak with simplicity." Either works. Go to a bar, sit on a stool, and listen. What will you hear? Stories. Speaking simply like a common man doesn't mean using a grade school vocabulary; it means drawing on knowledge and experience to give your thoughts substance (wisdom/complexity) and then expressing them as dynamic, causally connected events (common man/simplicity).

As we've said repeatedly, the typical mode of human communication is story. Its atypical side is the years of grueling education and hard-won experience that endow you with wisdom, so that when you speak, you have something to say others need to hear.

Visionaries, like Bezos, storify their entire enterprise. They communicate in story form in two directions: into the world and into the company. They use story outward to market and sell, and inward to shape executive thinking. Story (not data) is their tool to build teams, design products, analyze strategy, plan strategically, sell, service, and above all lead.

Once visionaries master story form, they teach the craft inside their entire company. In a future title, we will explore how this is done, how story can transform the inner life of an entire enterprise.

11

BUILDING AUDIENCE

Humanity's first stories were danced and chanted around the fire in caves, as tribal leaders passed their knowledge from generation to generation. Ancient civilizations inscribed their myths and legends on the walls of temples and pyramids, carving them in stone to be read for eons. Like the timeless epics of Homer and the beloved novels of Charles Dickens, wonderful stories are not just told, they're retold, again and again. Great storytelling attracts crowds into the future.

EARNED AUDIENCE

Consider the National Public Radio phenomenon *This American Life*. *TAL* broadcasts and podcasts nonfiction stories to a weekly audience of well over two million, both in the United States and abroad. Its many spin-offs include the film *The Informant* and the digital audio series *Serial*, which listeners have downloaded more than one hundred million times.[1] iTunes ranked

Serial's first-season podcasts number one for weeks on end, while the *New York Times, Mother Jones*, and many other publications spread the word in print.

Why? What explains the reach of these storified snippets of real life?

Three things: subject matter, execution, and replication of quality.

TAL's producer, Ira Glass, picks topics that fascinate people: parenting, dating, aging, music, science, sports, and the like. He then oversees the work of excellent storytellers, and finally, he keeps the show's storytelling top notch and has for twenty years. His audience knows they can count on compelling stories week after week.

Successful brand storytelling takes the same three steps: (1) Select topics that will fascinate your audience and satisfy them with insights and information they want and need, (2) hire the best creative talent you can find to dramatize these subjects into compelling stories, and (3) sustain that excellence over time. Skillfully execute these steps and, like *TAL*, your marketing will build a wide, faithful audience.

Above all, avoid the all-too-common budgeting mistake of allocating a tiny fraction to story creation and the rest to buying reach. At best, you'll end up with a couple of worthy tellings your prospective customers will quickly consume but then lose interest because you can't sustain the quality. At worst, you'll be stuck with a handful of badly told stories that'll cost serious media dollars to promote, bore people in the process, and damage your brand.

Internet-savvy marketers know that although persuasive storytelling takes the first big step to building an audience, it's amplification that finishes the job. So to launch a telling with immediate reach, they use organic search and social techniques that earn results without busting the budget.

LEVERAGING THE INTERNET'S DISCOVERY INFRASTRUCTURE

A torrent of content pours down the Internet each and every day: 1.7 million bloggers post entries across 1.03 billion websites, 39.6 million additional posts land on Tumblr, people share 24.8 million Instagram photos and tweet 247 million times.[2] Given this deluge, how can you make an impact?

To break through the noise, drive discovery, and retain your audience, you must pull the Internet's three levers of infrastructure: organic search, organic social, and email marketing/marketing automation.

Organic Reach: Search

When people today want an answer to a question, they jump straight to the Internet. The estimated 3.8 billion Internet users[3] search worldwide more than 175 billion times per month.[4] As we cited earlier, around 85 percent of the time people search, they do not click on the advertising that surrounds the content.[5] In 2016, marketers spent an estimated $81.6 billion on search advertising to capture that elusive 15 percent.[6] Based on these figures, we can sense that the market value of the organic search audience, people who click on content results rather than advertising, ranges between $400 and $800 billion.

How do we arrive at those figures? Simple. Searchers click on content results five to ten times more frequently than ads—the exact same searchers, searching for the exact same phrases that marketers pay millions to acquire through search ads.[7]

For the last two decades, marketers competing for this lucrative "organic" audience have called on search engine optimization (SEO). Early approaches to SEO began by identifying keywords and key phrases that were frequently searched. This provided a reliable way to identify what information people wanted. It also allowed companies to identify how their customers actually searched for information, learning which specific words and phrases people used in their discovery, and which were less common.

Armed with this information, marketers sought to "fool" search engines by "stuffing" the keywords and key phrases that people frequently searched into the content they published. "Keyword stuffing" succeeded at fooling relevance-based search engines like Lycos and AltaVista, and the quality of their search results suffered as a result. Increasingly, consumers would find poor-quality content (or even unrelated content, in egregious cases), stuffed with keywords, instead of the reliable information they sought.

Enter Google

In 1998, Google took a different approach to ranking search results, relying on a core mathematical algorithm called Page-Rank. With PageRank, Google could determine the authority of a given website based on the number of other websites that linked to it. Google used PageRank to prioritize content from more authoritative websites ahead of the content from lesser-known sites. Thanks to this new technique, and its ability to surface high-quality content more reliably, Google emerged as the world's dominant search engine.

Marketers were not easily beaten. Chasing billions of dollars in organic search value, they quickly adapted to the new rules of the game. They purchased and published links from other websites to their own so that their content would continue to appear at the top of Google results. Google forbade the practice and punished companies that it caught, but link-buying remained pervasive even through 2010.[8]

On February 23, 2011, Google introduced new algorithms collectively known as Panda,[9] soon followed by the additional algorithms Penguin and Hummingbird, which effectively changed the rules of the game. Google increasingly focused on content quality and engagement, until its algorithms now consider thousands of different factors when determining rank, updating them six hundred times a year.

Google's goal is simple: to provide the highest quality search results to its users so that it can remain the dominant search provider for decades to come. While SEO managers spend hours analyzing each new release for hints about what might provide a short-term advantage, you are better served by understanding Google's macro goals and crafting your strategy to match. To earn audience with organic search on a sustained basis, you should take one lesson from early SEO and another from the Storynomics model.

From SEO, you should learn to analyze search data to identify the topics that your customers care about and learn the many different ways they search for them. Google's AdWords and Trends tools can give you high-level insight into the answers to these questions. SEMrush and SpyFu offer more granular-level detail. Telling stories that your customers want and including the specific phrases that they use to search in your writing will drive organic search audience over time.

From the Storynomics model, you know that you must also invest in creating high-quality, original experiences for your customers and prospects. Google, Bing, and other search engines will continue to create technology that separates unique, high-quality experiences from copycat or low-quality ones. By delivering excellent stories to your customers, you not only put your best foot forward, but also increase the likelihood of earning audience from organic search.

Organic Reach: Social

People share the stories they like more frequently and more broadly than ever before with the help of social platforms like Facebook, Twitter, LinkedIn, Instagram, YouTube, Reddit, and Tumblr. On Facebook alone, people share content 4.75 billion times every day.[10] Around the world, 1.6 billion users log in to Facebook to see what their friends share, like, and comment on.[11]

The audience for the *Serial* podcast grew quickly through social mentions, as hundreds of thousands of listeners shared their passion. As *Serial's* success demonstrates, great stories, well told, hold the power to cascade broadly after they're discovered.

Companies once benefited from organic social cascade as well, earning significant reach through shares and likes on Facebook. However, as mentioned in chapter 10, late in 2014

Facebook changed its algorithms to sharply limit the organic reach of branded content in an effort to force marketers to spend more on Facebook ads.[12] In effect, Facebook removed content shared by brands from the Facebook feed, showing only user-shared content and paid placements from companies. Despite these changes, you can still earn significant audience reach through social. To do so, carefully select the creatives who will tell your stories.

Influencer Marketing, Done Right

Influencer marketing has existed for centuries, dating back to at least the 1760s when Josiah Wedgwood leveraged endorsements from the royals to establish the value of his brand in the minds of prospective customers.[13]

Since the advent of social media, where influencers can promote brand offerings directly to their followers, the practice has exploded. Marketers have raced to leverage socially connected experts, industry leaders, celebrities, and YouTube stars to sell their products.[14] In some cases, marketers simply send free goods to these stars, hoping they will feature them in an Instagram post or tweet. For influencers with larger audiences, brands will often pay a substantial fee as well. The *New York Times* reported, "Captiv8, a company that connects brands to influencers, says someone with three million to seven million followers can charge, on average, $187,500 for a post on YouTube, $75,000 for a post on Instagram or Snapchat and $30,000 for a post on Twitter. For influencers with 50,000 to 500,000 followers, the average is $2,500 for YouTube, $1,000 for Instagram or Snapchat and $400 for Twitter."[15]

The challenge with this approach: Many influencers choose to compromise their credibility by recommending products and experiences they do not actually know or use. Moreover, the same sophisticated consumers that see through the bragging and promising of advertising also understand the endorsement and product placement games.[16] This approach to influencer marketing is likely to suffer the same loss of consumer trust that advertising has as abuse after abuse trains influencer audiences to ignore their endorsements.[17] Fortunately, forward-thinking marketers have a better way to leverage this influence to connect with their customers.

When creating a content marketing experience for your customers, your first criteria for selecting contributors must be their domain expertise and their storytelling skills. But as you make your selection, recognize that your creatives can do far more than just tell stories for your brand. If you select contributors who are not only domain experts and good storytellers, but also recognized influencers on the topics you plan to address, those influencers can drive audience and bring credibility to your brand in the process.

Influencer marketing platforms provide influencers writing on any topic you may want to address from Polynesian travel to proteomics. These platforms not only measure the reach of each contributor, but how his content resonates, whether or not his audience shares, replies, or "likes" the stories he tells.

To earn organic social reach for your program, you need to: (1) Recruit contributors who bring audiences to your brand; (2) establish a compensation plan that rewards contributors for the total reach of their content, giving them an incentive to promote to their followers; and (3) measure which contributors and social channels drive the greatest audience to your content so that you can focus future assignments on these top performers. Because social algorithms on platforms like Facebook, Twitter, and LinkedIn do not filter brand stories when individual users share them, this approach enables you to earn meaningful organic social reach for your brand storytelling. Additionally, when you select influencers who are experts on the topics your customers care about and ask them to create the content your customers want, instead of shilling for your product, you deliver an authentic experience your audience enjoys and trusts.

The Stories They Tell

It's not just the stories we tell our customers, but the stories our customers tell about us. The Word of Mouth Marketing Association (WOMMA) found that the stories people tell to their friends about their experiences with companies drive 13 percent of all sales.[18] WOMMA also reported that customer stories become increasingly important to buyers when goods and services become more expensive (as shown in the chart below).

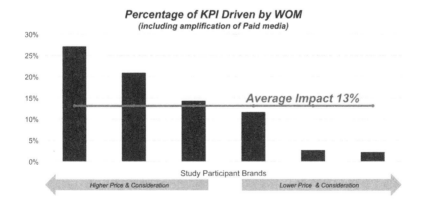

Percentage of KPI Driven by WOM
(including amplification of Paid media)

Their study underestimates the impact of word of mouth because it only measures the degree to which good word of mouth generates sales and doesn't capture the power of bad-mouthing to kill them. The lesson is clear: Today's consumer judges your performance and reviews it in public. Be certain yours is a five-star brand.

From Storyteller to Story-Maker

Mastercard chief marketing and communications officer Raja Rajamannar suggests that brands have an opportunity not just to create and tell stories to their customers, but also to involve their customers in the story itself. In a recent interview, Raja-mannar explained that technology has allowed us to create increasingly immersive experiences. Humanity moved from oral storytelling to written, then to film, radio, and television, adding sound effects and images that brought tales to life by showing, rather than telling, the story. More recently, virtual reality moves the audience member from an outside observer to someone sitting inside the story setting itself. This evolution inspired Rajamannar to ask, "How does our own story-telling evolve?" His answer turned Mastercard's "Priceless" traditional advertising campaign into an experiential marketing platform that today includes Priceless Cities and Priceless Surprises:

[In traditional stories] you make the audience live vicariously. In this case [the Priceless Cities Program], we say, "Can we make it his story?"

As an example, most of the credit card companies advertise, at the upper tier with a black card or platinum card, a concierge service. If you call them up to get Broadway tickets, you get the best seats of the house...and observe the play. If I want to put you *in* the story, I'll put you on stage and turn you into a living character.

We also created Priceless Surprises, whereby we literally took the age-old "surprise and delight" concept and made it an always-on program. Mastercard creates unique, unexpected moments in the lives of our cardholders. These moments come in all sizes, from having singer Ellie Goulding drop in during a recording session for two young artists[19] to giving a bonus Magnolia Bakery cupcake when a cardholder buys a first. These surprises, regardless of scope, have one thing in common: They serve as inciting incidents in the lives of cardholders, inspiring them to retell the story they've actually lived.[20]

The day after Mastercard launched the first Priceless Surprise with Justin Timberlake in 2014, Rajamannar received a call from Twitter CEO Dick Costolo, saying Mastercard had hit a nerve center. Twitter was lighting up with mentions of the Timberlake surprise, with users sharing the brand story throughout their networks. Since then, Mastercard has delivered more than six hundred thousand Priceless Surprises around the world, driving billions of stories to be told and retold by their customers on social media.

Bringing Audience Back

When you offer useful and entertaining stories, your audience can't wait for new material to arrive. To maximize your return on brand storytelling, enable your audience to subscribe to your storytelling experience using your email marketing, marketing automation, or customer relationship management platforms. Sending recommended stories brings audience members back more frequently, enabling you to build stronger relationships. More frequent visits will increase social sharing of your stories, helping you reach their friends and colleagues.

Personalized Recommendations

When you catch up with old friends over drinks, you subconsciously select the stories from your repertoire that you believe will interest them the most. Your mind considers everything you know about them, your shared interests, and prioritizes things that have happened that they're unlikely to have heard before. As a result, you have a better conversation, more entertaining or edifying than if you had just shared everything you'd learned since you last connected. Take the same approach toward each member of your audience to build stronger relationships.

A 2013 research study commissioned by Janrain found that "74 percent get frustrated with websites when content ... appear[s] that [has] nothing to do with their interests."[21] Yet even though 77 percent of marketers realize that personalizing experiences is crucial to success, 60 percent of them fail to do it in real time.[22] Many attempt to match archetype personas with the people they represent, configuring a different email for each persona, but still fall far short of what the individual wants and needs.

New artificial intelligence (AI) platforms allow you to move past the persona to the truly personal. Technologies from companies including Skyword, LiftIgniter, and OneSpot build anonymous profiles of each of your audience members, then use sophisticated algorithms to select the right stories from your library for each person, based on what they have found most compelling in the past.

AI-based recommendations can increase the rate at which your audience consumes additional stories by as much as 50 percent over the tag-based recommendations that most websites use. Using personalized story recommendations in your nurturing emails can drive a 50 to 120 percent increase in click-throughs from those emails.[23] In short, telling the right story to the right person drives better business results.

Paid Amplification

Once you've created an outstanding experience for your audience and personalized it for each audience member, you will want to maximize your audience reach.

Building organic reach via search and social drives the highest ROI, but to do it at scale can take six to eighteen months. Additionally, if you use only organic methods to build audience, you will suboptimize the impact of your brand storytelling. To accelerate audience growth and maximize total reach, paid promotion offers a faster, broader path. *Serial*'s first podcasts, for example, drew a modest initial listenership, but when *This American Life* promoted the show, hundreds of thousands of public radio listeners tuned in, and once hooked, they kept coming back for more. Similarly, to build a seed audience quickly or to drive people to high-gloss content that you create occasionally, call on paid amplification.

David Beebe cut his teeth as a producer at Disney/ABC, where he spent more than six years overseeing television and digital show production. In mid-2014, Beebe recognized the coming shift from ad-centric to story-centric marketing and left the media world to become vice president, global creative and content marketing, at Marriott International. At Marriott, David Beebe oversees content efforts to launch new brands, build brand awareness, and "put heads in beds."

While consistent publishing of *Marriott Traveler*[24] earns most of the brand's traffic via search, Beebe provides media support behind their high-gloss work with short films such as *French Kiss* and *Two Bellmen Three*.

Beebe explained, "We target the brands' audiences using all of the data we have. We start by identifying business travelers who [have] engaged with us at JW, mashing our data with Google and YouTube's data.

"We then run all of our films as pre-roll ads, as TrueView.[25] We put media spend on them. So someone goes to YouTube to watch something completely different, and then they are presented with this ad. But it's actually an interesting piece of content and they get sucked into it. On YouTube, there was an 80 percent completion rate of people watching the films, and YouTube told us they'd never seen that before with advertising."[26]

Smart paid amplification begins by looking at your organic results. What stories earned the greatest audience? These statistics will show where the market demand was highest for your offering. What stories had the highest rates of engagement and social cascade? These stats will show where your stories connected with your audience and delivered meaningful value. Armed with this information, consider content discovery networks and targeted social campaigns to build audience. Content discovery networks like Taboola, Outbrain, Nativo, TripleLift, and media companies like Yahoo and Time, promote brand content on media websites, then charge for each visit they drive to your content. More recently, real-time bidding advertising networks have started to do the same, distributing content in the spaces that used to be reserved exclusively for ads. Facebook offers powerful tools for targeting the stories you craft to the readers and viewers most likely to enjoy them. There are so many options available today for content amplification that marketers often turn to media buyers to manage and optimize that amplification for them. For those that want to manage their own buying, we recommend amplification management platforms like Zemanta or Reactor Media, which optimize content amplification campaigns across many of the networks mentioned above. Zemanta also enables marketers to measure cost/goal achievement, and will automatically optimize their amplification spend to focus on the most cost-effective channels.

Although these cost-per-click models are similar to the paid promotion used by novices to promote their native advertising campaigns, there is one major difference: Here, you are acquiring audience members that you have an opportunity to retain, instead of renting them on a one-off basis.

How much should you spend on amplification? Beebe

explained, "We try to put in place a 2:1 ratio. If we spent $500,000 on a film, we spend $250,000 on the marketing and promotion of it...That's no different from the world that I came from in TV, but there you would spend not just the budget of a show, but maybe double or triple that marketing the thing."

Your brand may not invest in storytelling on the same scale that Marriott does. The benefits of amplification in driving larger audience, faster than you might earn organically, hold true at any scale. Once you have created an experience that engages your audience, consider amplifying that experience to maximize your return on investment.

Any of the above amplification options can drive audience to your stories. Measuring cost per visit and whether that audience sticks around, returns, or shares your content will allow you to choose the option that works best. The next critical step is to tie this measurement to true return on investment. We'll explore how to do that in chapter 13.

12

STORIFIED SALES

In our website-to-us world, marketing, not sales efforts, drives everyday purchases . . . literally to our doorstep. When we leave home to shop, we enter the even more impersonal universe of self-service. We touchpad a fast-food order; fill our own Slurpee cups; drop groceries in a pushcart, then self-check, self-pay, self-bag.

It's not until prices reach big-ticket numbers that transactions revert to the time-honored and more personal relationship of buyer/seller. To get face-to-face with customers, however, a sales team needs leads. In business-to-business (B2B) industries, for example, marketing typically drives just 25 to 30 percent of all sales leads.[1] Direct outreach by sales personnel accounts for 45 to 47 percent, and the balance of 24 to 29 percent comes by way of referrals, partners, and other sources.

Today's B2B salespeople come armed with better tools for identifying, contacting, and following up with prospects than ever before. A growing list of sales enablement tools allow you to find prospects (RainKing, ZoomInfo), send messages, share presentations, track when recipients open what you send

(Yesware, ClearSlide), and even analyze the personalities of the people you are trying to contact (Crystal Knows).

Yet CSO Insights found that over the past seven years, companies averaged just 84 percent of their sales targets, while their sales executives only met 59 percent of their quotas.[2] Why? What to blame? Improperly set targets? Economic headwinds? Product performance? Any or all could be to blame, but consistent underachievement over time across the landscape suggests something more. The problem begins with antiquated sales strategies.

THE NUMBERS GAME

When devising strategy, most sales executives focus on the quantity of connections made instead of the quality of those connections. They play a numbers game, setting monthly targets for calls or prospecting emails because history has taught them that making X number of calls will lead to Y number of meetings, and holding Y meetings will result in Z deals.

Trained in this approach and armed with new technologies, young sellers pound their phones and keyboards. They may or may not reach their call quotas, but it won't matter either way because they rarely hook attention whenever anyone answers.

Consider the buyer's point of view. How many emails have you received this week alone that started with bragging and promising or, worse yet, an immediate request for your time? A sales rep who writes, "May I have just fifteen minutes of your time?" may as well ask for $50 out of your wallet. Now ask yourself, how many of those emails do you return?

Sending out thousands of emails may trigger a sale or two,

but just as interrupt advertising abuses consumers, interrupt emails rile B2B buyers and leave them numb. Yet if you walk down the hall and review the emails your sales team is sending, chances are they are sending the same kind of messages that you ignore. There must be a better way for sales to hook customer attention.

And when they do, there must be a better way to hold it. After playing the numbers game, if and when a sales rep secures a meeting, she inevitably illustrates her demo on PowerPoint or Keynote. Her pitch, almost without exception, runs a rhetorical argument for her product, bolstered by data converted into graphs and tables, spliced here and there with upbeat images overlaid with motivational quotes, all trying to prove her thesis.

After the demo, common practice calls for the sales rep to leave something with the client, usually a print piece known in the trade as a "leave behind." This document adds nothing; it simply repeats the presentation, describing, praising, and arguing for the company and its products yet again. As you might guess, the failure rate of this gesture nears 100 percent. Save the trees.

DESIRE TRIGGERS SALES

No one takes any action (let alone makes a pricy purchase) unless he feels, consciously or subconsciously, that the action he has chosen is either his best choice or, at the very least, his only choice. People follow where desire leads.

What will a buyer buy? To motivate a high-cost purchase, a sales pitch not only must hook and hold the buyer's rational self, but also must simultaneously engage his feeling self so that he *wants* to buy. And the best way, perhaps the only way, to intrigue a buyer's emotional curiosity is to tell a story that dramatizes his struggle to get what he wants.

STORY TO THE RESCUE

This new sales world demands new tactics, and the eight stages of storytelling arm you with a targeted strategy. For a B2C salesperson, gathering storytelling insight about a customer before he walks in the door is next to impossible, but the storytelling process can shape your interactions. Put to work in B2B sales, the eight stages build three key storified moments: (1) a powerful hook secures a meeting with a prospective client, (2) a relatable, dramatic story arc grips attention and emotionally links the client to your product or service, and (3) a compelling story climax closes the sale.

For these moments to succeed, you need to thoroughly research each stage of storytelling. You need to picture the industry and identify protagonists, inciting incidents, objects of desire, and actions and reactions. Having this backstory at your fingertips will empower you to communicate and connect with your clients. So let's go through these stages with an eye toward B2B sales.

STAGE ONE: TARGETS

Long before it makes a call or sends an email, a top sales team always conducts market research. In a story-driven strategy research becomes Stage One. This first step identifies the target audience, target need, and target action. Begin by laying out the industry's history. Sketch its story arcs of dynamic change. Identify each downturn and upturn, analyze what went right, and most importantly, what went wrong, for the secret to sales success is discovery of the specific client need that hides somewhere in those negative turns. The target action, of course, is the client's purchase of your product or service to fulfill her need.

For example, let's say your company sells a cloud-based electronic health records (EHR) platform to hospitals and other medical providers. Your customers use your platform to record patient data in a standardized way, ensure all tests and records are captured, share patient information with the patients themselves and with their other providers, and keep that data secure.

Your prospects understand some of the benefits of your offering, but your research showed they are concerned about its implications. On one hand, switching from paper to electronic records would increase the access medical professionals have to patient histories. Your systems have the potential to reduce errors and omissions in medical treatment, and if employed as designed, they could significantly reduce costs over time.

On the other hand, research also reveals that your prospects are concerned about making this change. How would your systems be added to their medical facilities? What training would medical professionals need to use them? How could they keep the information private and secure? If records were more portable, would patients move to other providers more frequently?

Now you know where it hurts. Answer these questions with an up-ending story, and the sale is made.

STAGE TWO: SUBJECT MATTER

Step 1: Core Value

Regular storytelling often mixes and merges core values. But in the purpose-told sales story, the binary value is obvious: success/failure. This core value's positive/negative charge regulates business life from the dry cleaners down the street to multinationals in New York, London, and Beijing.

Subsets of success/failure, such as innovation/imitation, efficiency/inefficiency, risk/safety, and leader/follower, shape specific pitches to specific clients. But ultimately, they all relate to whether or not a business succeeds.

In our EHR example, market research would uncover two major pieces of legislation that changed the industry landscape: the 2009 American Recovery and Reinvestment Act and the Patient Protection and Affordable Care Act, often referred to as the ACA or "Obamacare."

The American Recovery and Reinvestment Act was an $831 billion stimulus package designed to help the US economy recover more quickly from the economic downturn caused by the mortgage crisis. Part of that stimulus was set aside to modernize health care, providing incentives to public and private health care providers that could demonstrate "meaningful use" of EHR systems.[3] Those that did not adopt EHR systems by 2014 would face penalties and see Medicaid and Medicare reimbursement levels drop over time. Your prospective customers suddenly had a very real reason to adopt your technology or that of your competitor.

The ACA, when adopted in 2010, added a new twist to the industry. The Congressional Budget Office estimated that twenty-one million Americans obtained health insurance due to the ACA, twelve million were added to the Medicare rolls, and an additional nine million received federal means-based subsidies.[4]

In addition to increasing the number of insured Americans, the ACA also began to change how providers are paid for their services. Instead of being compensated for the tests run and treatment provided, which gave providers incentives to test and treat more often than may be necessary, the ACA begins to shift compensation to reward successful outcomes, starting in 2018. This means medical providers have incentives to run the right tests and offer treatments most likely to deliver the results.

From an EHR perspective, this change meant that systems had to be adapted or changed to track and record outcomes, correlate them to tests and treatments offered, and then provide more robust analytics. For the sake of our example, let's say our sales executive reaches out in the future after both of these laws have been put in effect.

Step 2: PROTAGONIST

A purpose-driven sales story stars its client. You'll waste time and money if you focus on your product or company. Based on your big picture of prospective clients, draw up a general idea of your protagonist—the buyer with whom you will ideally meet. Once you zero in on the specific companies and people, go back and do more homework about both so you can understand what challenges (forces of antagonism) your protagonist faces.

In our EHR example, the target customer is the medical provider's CEO and/or the hospital administrator. Physicians and nursing staff may influence the decision.

Step 3: Setting

Like a great storyteller, you need an expert's knowledge of the world of your potential clients. Zero in on the particulars: a company's history, its position in the industry (leader, challenger, laggard), the markets where the company competes, the power politics of that space (regulations, consumer sentiment, key suppliers, key distributors), the value proposition the company presents to its customers and how it tries to sell it. Note that you should revisit the details of core value, protagonist, and setting all along the way as you gather more information about your prospective clients.

In our EHR example, in addition to the legislative changes mentioned above, our sales representative notes that medical providers have been consolidating to create efficiencies of scale. Hospital groups merge and acquire specialty practices in the region.

STAGE THREE: INCITING INCIDENT

This stage gives you the information you need to prioritize the prospect list you've been fleshing out in the first two stages.

Of the companies on your list ask, "What is the present state of balance in this prospect's operation? Is the industry that surrounds it in stasis or shifting? If so, which way does it arc? Rising? Falling? Is the company itself growing? Shrinking? Holding steady?"

If a prospect is clearly on the rise or clearly falling, something happened in its relatively recent past to trigger that change. In other words, an inciting incident rocked this company, reversed its fortunes, and launched its present-day story.

A company out of balance tends to take risks (perhaps buying something new and innovative from you) in the hope of rebalance, or even a turnaround. So take your research to greater depth by determining what the inciting incident was, how it happened, and what exactly tipped the company's scales. If a company's inciting incident has caused negative change, then it's in a life-and-death struggle to survive. They will be strong prospects, so long as your product or service can turn the tide.

That's not to say that companies experiencing positive value change (new capital, major new accounts, or the like) are out of reach. Events that cause positive value change inevitably trigger a cascade of challenges. A major innovation (*positive*) may mean a company suddenly finds itself understaffed (*negative*), lacking inventory (*negative*), or with an exhausted team (*negative*). Growth might lead to negatives such as struggles to hire talent, grooming staff for growth, balancing focus between existing and new products, and balancing today's profits against investments that will drive tomorrow's. If your prospect is savoring a recent success, hook her curiosity by noting the possibility of a negative turn or two just around the corner.

Next come companies that haven't recently experienced an

inciting incident, but the market expects one soon. If you sell IT security, for example, financial services companies that have not been hacked, but are viewed in the industry as ripe targets for hackers, would make strong prospects. Companies that have been hacked and lived to tell it know the dangers and will always want the most up-to-date technology and processes possible. As companies like these prepare for change, they become the next-most-likely-to-purchase group. Once again, in evaluating such companies, ask which direction the inciting incident on the horizon will turn their fortunes.

As for companies in relative stasis and expected to remain so for the foreseeable future, put them at the bottom of your list. They are least likely to close, but may take up time and resources that are better focused elsewhere.

Now rank your prospects. The best strategy orders them by the inciting incidents in their recent corporate stories. Put the high-yield, high-value prospects at the top and the low-yield, low-value possibilities at the bottom:

1. Companies that have experienced a negative inciting incident.
2. Companies that have experienced a positive inciting incident.
3. Companies preparing for a negative inciting incident.
4. Companies preparing for a positive inciting incident.
5. Companies in balance with no prospect of change in either direction.

Returning to our EHR example, in this case our sales representative may identify and prioritize practices that have recently announced an acquisition. The sales rep would recognize that newly merged companies must combine EHR platforms, and that creates a unique moment when they might consider switching to his company.

Alternatively, the rep may focus on companies that are starting to transition from treatment-based compensation to outcome-based compensation from Medicare. This fundamental shift in compensation creates a unique inciting incident that throws hospital operations out of balance. For the purposes of our example, we'll focus on this group going forward.

STAGE FOUR: OBJECT OF DESIRE

Look at each prospect and identify the person you will contact—that's your protagonist. Based on the inciting incident that has thrown the company out of balance, dig deeper to determine your protagonist's object of desire. What is her company's focused need—the thing (a new product) or situation (a greater share of market)—that it believes will right its ship?

From crisis to crisis, from department to department, the exact nature of a company's object of desire is often so unclear top executives can't figure it out. As a salesperson, however, you cannot take a step forward until you do. Once you gain this insight, decide how your product or service meets that client need.

In our EHR example, the hospital CEO's object of desire should be crystal: He wants to transition his hospital into the outcomes-based framework without loss of profit.

Next, compose your email's subject line or first sentence to acknowledge your prospect's inciting incident and resulting object of desire.

```
Subject: Shifting to Outcomes-Based Compensation
Dear [HOSPITAL CEO]:
    The coming shift from treatment-based to
outcomes-based compensation requires significant
change in hospital operations. In an increasingly
competitive environment, making this shift suc-
cessfully can determine the difference between
long-term success and failure for [HOSPITAL SYS-
TEM]. To begin that transformation, you will need
to correlate tests and treatments that have been
run across your system with the actual results
they deliver.
```

STAGE FIVE: THE FIRST ACTION

Be aware that the company will no doubt have tried to cope with its inciting incident, but its tactics obviously didn't work, or your prospect wouldn't be reading your email. Be sure to research the actions your client has already taken and why and how they failed. Use this knowledge to further frame your outreach and avoid the enormous embarrassment of having your solution be something they have already tried. In our EHR example, your email may continue:

```
I know that you installed our competitor's plat-
form locally in 2011 and that your IT team has
been working to upgrade it with the latest ver-
sion over the past year.
```

STAGE SIX: THE FIRST REACTION

Now let's say that the client's first actions to achieve her object of desire failed because of unforeseen forces of antagonism blocking her way. Your final piece of research, therefore, identifies these failed attempts and the forces that thwarted them.

Where did the negative forces come from? From what level of reality? Were they physical forces such as natural disasters? Social forces such as competitors? Government agencies? Technological revolutions? Personal rivalries between executives? Inner conflicts within executives? Some combination of the above? Exactly what stops her from reaching her object of desire? What has nailed her corporate life to a negative floor?

Your email to the hospital CEO might then continue:

```
But because our competitor's software is
installed locally on your own servers and
requires that additional client software be
installed on every PC in your hospital, I rec-
ognize that this upgrade requires a great deal
```

of time. Unfortunately, in the months since your
team began that upgrade, Medicare has altered
how it plans to measure and quantify outcomes.
That upgrade will be out of date the day it is
complete.

STAGE SEVEN: THE SECOND ACTION

Having learned everything the prospect has experienced to
date, especially the way the world reacted to the company's
latest effort to rebalance, you ride to the rescue. This is where
all your research comes together in the story you tell your prospective client and earns your face-to-face meeting.

Fortunately, our EHR platform is cloud-based.
If you shift to our solution, your IT team will
not need to upgrade servers or change software
in every exam room and nurse's station. And our
platform will always be current, conforming to
constantly changing health care regulations and
policies.

At this point, having demonstrated knowledge of your customer's story, what threw his life out of balance, his object of
desire, and his failed attempts to achieve it, you have made him
anxious to hear your solution. How much more likely is the
hospital CEO to accept your request for a call if he receives this
email, rather than one that simply requests his time so you can
talk about your company?

Your story should reveal all of your in-depth understanding by referencing the critical inciting incident, the unfulfilled need it inspired, the company's current dilemma, and how your product or service will help the company fulfill that need.

Be sure to select the specific capabilities of your offering that will drive a positive change for your immediate customer. If your product is multifaceted, dramatize only those facets relevant to the client. When you recite everything your product can do, you sound like a braggart and lose credibility. Beware of side stories about how your product has worked for your current prospect's competitors. Those, too, may cost you credibility as your client begins to wonder whose side you're on.

Bear in mind that companies don't decide to buy products or hire services, people do. To close a sale, craft events that connect emotionally with your decision maker.

STAGE EIGHT: THE CLIMACTIC REACTION

Once you have your meeting or call, you'll have an opportunity to retell a similar story, this time featuring a customer who faced a situation similar to our hospital CEO's, but succeeded due to your solution. Close that story with the upending climax that overcame the negative forces that opposed your successful client, achieved his object of desire, and restored balance to his company's fortunes. Your prospect will see that, as soon as he makes his own purchase, this future victory awaits.

Thus, the sales story closes with a happy ending.

13

-NOMICS

To transform your marketing from ad-centric to story-centric, you'll need enthusiastic buy-ins from the C-suites. To excite your corporate team, simply show them that story makes money. Then back it up with data.

Proof of storytelling's financial impact calls for the collection and analysis of key data, but exactly what you measure depends on your core goal. Do you use story to differentiate your brand from your competitor? Expand brand awareness? Build brand affinity? Develop leads for your sales force? Identify likely purchasers? All the above? Your answers determine how you gauge success, but at the end of the day, one metric fortifies the rest.

MEASURING BRAND SUCCESS

The ultimate factor is margin growth. Companies that build positive relationships with the broadest reach of prospective customers charge the greatest differentiated margin for their goods and services. In other words, underlying costs being the same, a much-loved brand sells virtually the same thing as its competitors, but because it's loved, it charges more and thus earns more.

Reach due to amplification-for-hire distorts the spontaneous connection between you and your audience, so to measure the power of your stories to build brand affinity, focus on three key metrics: organic reach, audience composition, and engagement.

KEY CONTENT METRICS

Tools like Google Analytics or Adobe Marketing Cloud collect key content and reach metrics. With them, you can track how many unique people visit your content, how much time they spend consuming it, and whether they pass it along. Platforms like SEMrush or SpyFu for search, or TrackMaven or ONZU for social, enable you to compare your brand's performance against that of your competitors.

Using public data from SEMrush, we can examine the success of Colgate's Oral Care Center. According to SEMrush, Colgate's content now earns 2.7 million visits each month from more than three hundred thousand keywords that prospective Colgate customers search to develop good dental habits or to learn about dental health challenges. SEMrush estimates that if Colgate had to pay for that same number of visits with Google AdWords, their marketing spend would cost another $93 million annually.[1] Without a single brag or promise, Colgate's Oral Care earns customer attention at a fraction of that cost by understanding their consumers' needs and providing what they want.

MEASURING MARKET SUCCESS

If you market directly to consumers (B2C), measure your success by using the same three metrics suggested above: reach (total audience size), audience composition (who actually reads the content), and engagement (time spent on content, frequency of return, and social sharing). You can measure this information using content marketing platforms like Skyword and Kapost,[2] or analytics platforms like Google Analytics and Adobe Analytics. If your company transacts business online, Google and Adobe can also be configured to measure conversions of sales or subscribers.

By integrating content marketing and analytics platforms, sales success can be tracked to specific topics, authors, distribution channels—even down to an individual story. Armed with this insight, you can shape your program to maximize sales or any other goal that you track.

Overstock, for example, analyzed the ROI on its storified marketing spend and reported that 70 percent of readers who visit O.info, its storytelling site, then shop at Overstock.com, its ecommerce site. In fact, post-story visitors convert at seven times the rate of visitors acquired elsewhere and spend an average of 35 percent more on each transaction.

Once you track your brand's storytelling through to sales, you can compare that ROI to your advertising and other marketing spends to see how they compare. When it's clear that your storified branding delivers better ROI, it's time to shift your resources.

If you market for a B2B company, integrate your content marketing platform with a marketing automation system such as Marketo, Eloqua, Pardot, or Unica. This link helps you identify which stories generate which leads, and, in turn, how these leads engage with and share your stories. Add to that system a sales automation platform like Salesforce, and you'll know exactly when your story-generated leads result in sales. Measuring lead volume, quality, size, and close rate lets you identify the leads inspired by your storified marketing versus what's coming down the rest of your pipeline. In other words, you'll know exactly what topics, creatives, media types, and channels work and which do not.

MEASURING SALES SUCCESS

In chapter 12, we advocated the use of story to qualify sales prospects versus the ratios-driven strategy of X calls = Y meetings = Z sales. We believe that the latter technique wastes your sales reps' time on the least likely, while they burn through the most promising. So although numerical systems should not determine your out-going strategy, they can usefully measure your in-coming success.

To weigh the impact of your storified pitches, ask yourself these questions:

- **Sales Calls Versus Meetings:** At the outset, do our inquiries hook our prospects? To find out, measure the ratio of your storified emails and calls to the meetings they generate.

- **Initial Meetings Versus Proposals:** How well does our storified qualification system rank our leads? To answer that, measure your ratio of initial meetings to sales proposals.
- **Close Rate:** When my team pitches face-to-face with prospects, do they tell engaging sales stories? You'll see your close rate the moment you measure your ratio of proposals to sales.
- **ASP:** Finally, have our storified methods raised our average selling price (ASP)? Are we getting greater value for our core offering and maximizing upsells? To know, simply compare previous ASPs to your current ASP; the numbers will tell the story.

Sales automation platforms like Salesforce and Microsoft Dynamics, or sales clouds by SAP and Oracle, allow you to track sales activity. Business intelligence layers, such as Insight-Squared, show you key ratios and trends at a glance. These systems also compare individual sales reps against your company average and identify your most and least effective storytellers.

Transforming marketing and sales from rhetoric-centric to story-centric requires initiative, leadership, and sustained investment. To succeed, you must consistently measure the metrics appropriate to your strategic goals. Once you see progressive improvement, you can confidently fund your storytelling into the future.

Conclusion
TOMORROW

The future started yesterday: Two centuries of print advertising built the ad-supported media model that underwrote our radio and television networks. By the 1990s, commercials peaked in selling power, ad-soaked broadcast reached the saturation point, and the slow, inevitable decline of advertising soon followed.

The future of brand storytelling will no doubt trace a similar arc. As this technique matures, the scope and sources of capital available to storytelling will shift strongly in its favor. With these new resources, storytellers will accelerate the demise of the ad-driven model, while they inspire innovation in radical media such as augmented reality, virtual reality, and gaming. These ideas will in turn inspire technologies we can't yet imagine that will give more people more time in their day to consume more storified knowledge and entertainment. Done right, brand storytelling will not only power muscular business outcomes, but give marketers unimagined opportunities.

THE COMING CREATIVE RENAISSANCE

What will happen when companies shift a major chunk of the $600 billion they spend on advertising to sustained brand storytelling? First, marketers will no longer have to rent audiences.

In the old world of traditional media, companies spent a tiny minority of their budget on creating compelling advertising, then the vast majority on buying distribution for those ads. Over time, this lopsided allocation made media buying agencies many times larger than the creative agencies that actually produced the ads.

But in a world where thousands, maybe millions, share stories they love, the balance reverses: Tomorrow's story-driven marketers will invest the balance of their budgets in creating stories and a declining share in distributing them. This envisions a brilliant future for creatives.

Season one of *Westworld* and season six of *Game of Thrones* cost HBO about $100 million[1] each, while the first ten episodes of Netflix's *The Crown* topped $130 million. In fact, when Netflix added up all the budgets for its 2016 roster of original programming—*House of Cards*, *Orange Is the New Black*, and so on—the total hit $6 billion.[2]

Those numbers may seem large until you realize that in the same year Procter & Gamble spent $9.7 billion in advertising.[3] Now imagine the selling power that brands like P&G would have if they invested in the HBO/Netflix level of writing, acting, directing, and production values for their marketing stories...

Creatives who work with brands need to align their craft with their patron, the CMO. The stories they craft must hook, hold, and pay off, but their ultimate goal is a positive, measurable business result. Creatives need to understand how marketers think; CMOs need to break away from campaign-driven approaches and think in story arcs.

THE STREAMING SCREEN

The future of TV is apps.

—Tim Cook, CEO, Apple Inc.

On September 9, 2015, Apple CEO Tim Cook introduced the newest version of Apple TV. The device does more than allow consumers to access television and movies from Apple or watch shows via Netflix, Hulu, and HBO. It allows anyone anywhere to fill their train ride, elliptical workout, or evening relaxation with the stories they desire.

Today, if a financial planning company like BlackRock wants to reach its customers before they head for work each morning, it buys time on CNBC's *Squawk Box* and inserts its ads in the breaks. Now suppose BlackRock produced a high-quality video program filled with compelling, current business news stories and streamed it directly to consumers.

Instead of interrupting their customers with advertising, BlackRock could integrate products, such as their customized portfolio tracking and trading tools, into the show and create a one-stop shop for their customers. With that, *Business News by*

BlackRock would work like product placement in feature films, only far better.

THE NEW NEW MEDIA

The old new media simply replicate broadcast TV on digital platforms; the new new media leap into the great beyond of virtual and augmented realities. "I'm not interested in the novelty factor," said virtual reality (VR) filmmaker Chris Milk, "I'm interested in . . . a medium that could be more powerful than cinema, than theatre, than literature, than any other medium we've had before to connect one human being to another."[4]

Reality-altering devices sold by Samsung Gear, HTC VIVE, and PlayStation VR turn consumers into protagonists of video games played out in virtual realities or into active observers of VR documentaries. In both cases, technology hugely heightens the story's events—and with it the audience's experience. For the CMO, VR and augmented reality (AR) will extend marketing reach into an otherwise unreachable block of consumers and impact them with stories told in never-seen-before settings. In fact, this medium's potential to market to gamers and other seekers of peak experience prompted Facebook to acquire Oculus for $2 billion.

HEAD OUT ON THE HIGHWAY

Why Tesla and Mercedes invest in driverless cars is obvious, but why are Google and Apple doing the same? According to the US Census, 139 million American workers spend an average of fifty-two minutes driving back and forth to work each day. To put that amount of time in perspective, the *Washington Post* computed that in 2014 American commuters spent 1.8 trillion minutes in commute. This equals 29.6 billion hours, 1.2 billion days, or 3.4 million years.

Therefore, the most powerful technological innovation of the coming decade won't change the story experience; it will instead convert drive time to story time. While today's drivers may enjoy podcasts as they navigate traffic, tomorrow's will binge-watch their favorite Netflix series, or perhaps one created by an innovative brand, as their self-driving cars carry them on their most efficient route.

For Google and Apple, the self-driving car represents a daily interface with 139 million captive consumers in the United States alone. Moreover, these new geo-located consumer connections may influence consumers as they drive toward potential points of purchase.

NO TURNING BACK

In the past, televisions colonized the living room, sending radios in retreat to the dashboard. Now that always-on, on-demand, ad-free programming streams to our smart screens, there's no turning back to broadcast commercials. Executives who pine for the "good old days" of interrupt advertising are future-blind. The consumer shift to ad-free media will only accelerate, and so the brand shift to story-driven models must fast-track with them . . . or die. This transformation will not come easily.

Creating a successful story-centric strategy requires risk, trial, error, and persistent effort over time. So CMOs face the arduous task of educating their teams on the cultural shifts that demand story-centric marketing, the techniques of story design, why story fits the consumer's mind, the tactics of storified marketing, and how the purpose-told story motivates purchases.

That said, marketers who make Storynomics work have an extraordinary opportunity. Instead of wasting millions on interrupt advertising, what if you could thrive in your business and at the same time do good in this wanting world? Suppose you were to stop bragging about your products and promising fictional futures, and instead tell stories that enrich your audiences with humanistic insight? Suppose you could build brand affinity with your target audience, and at the same time touch their hearts in ways that deepen their lives?

Take inspiration from works like *Dove Real Beauty Sketches*, Always's #LikeAGirl, and Ariel's #ShareTheLoad[5] and create stories you deeply believe in. Then tell them with a double-edged purpose: brand appreciation and social change.

You, the readers of this book, will shape the future of brand storytelling, so we extend the same advice that thousands of the world's best fiction writers have been given at the McKee Story Seminars:

Write the Truth.

NOTES

Introduction: The Marketing Crisis

1. While some of this shift may be attributed to the convenience of on-demand viewing, the dominance of ad-free Netflix over Hulu, which used interrupt advertising in its first iteration, clearly demonstrates that consumers reject the ad model.
2. Dennis F. Herrick, *Media Management in the Age of Giants* (Albuquerque: University of New Mexico Press, 2012).
3. For "What's the Matter with Owen: Hammer," please see www.storynom ics.com/resources/ge; for "Misunderstood" by Apple, please see www .storynomics.com/resources/applemisunderstood; and for "Click, Baby, Click" by Adobe, please see www.storynomics.com/resources/adobe.

Chapter One: Advertising, A Story of Addiction

1. http://www.pbs.org/benfranklin/l3_wit_master.html.
2. The world's first radio news program was broadcast in Detroit, Michigan, on August 31, 1920, by BMK. One year later, on October 8, 1921, the first live sports broadcast was made by KDKA in Pittsburgh. The city listened as the Pitt Panthers defeated the West Virginia Mountaineers (21–13) in college football. Beer commercials were sure to follow. And they did.
3. http://adage.com/article/btob/assessing-dvrs-impact-tv-ads/263248.
4. http://www.wsj.com/articles/cable-tv-shows-are-sped-up-to-squeeze -in-more-ads-1424301320?mod=WSJ_hpp_MIDDLENexttoWhats NewsThird.

5. YouTube, founded in 2005, leveraged broadband to allow anyone, anywhere to publish digital video. By July 2015, more than four hundred hours of video were being uploaded to YouTube every minute (http://www.reelseo.com/vidcon-2015-strategic-insights-tactical-advice). Every month, one billion people, representing more than one-third of worldwide Internet users, watch YouTube videos. The company reports that "every day people watch hundreds of millions of hours on YouTube and generate billions of views." To put this in perspective with traditional media offerings, YouTube on mobile alone reaches more people ages eighteen through thirty-four, and thirty-five through forty-nine, than any cable network in the United States (https://www.youtube.com/yt/press/statistics.html).

6. Marketers found they could target advertisements much more effectively online. Instead of targeting a show's audience when only a portion of those viewers represented potential customers, marketers could zero in on individuals based on social profiles and viewing habits, focusing their advertising spend where it counted.

7. https://www.emarketer.com/Article/US-Digital-Ad-Spending-Surpass-TV-this-Year/1014469.

8. https://www.wsj.com/articles/ad-spending-growth-to-slow-significantly-in-2017-1480914002.

9. Netflix launched its website in 1999, allowing consumers to create lists of their favorite movies. But it turned to the US Postal Service to deliver those movies as DVDs to customers for eight more years. Consumers liked having movies and television shows available, ad-free, at home at all times. By 2007, Netflix was one of the largest customers of USPS and had shipped DVDs to subscribers more than one billion times (http://www.institutionalinvestor.com/article/3494635/banking-and-capital-markets-corporations/netflix-is-creating-a-cordless-nightmare-for-traditional-media.html#.VmVgbeMrKRs).

10. http://www.theverge.com/2017/1/18/14312826/netflix-earnings-q4-2016-7-million-new-subscribers.

11. http://www.wsj.com/articles/netflixs-global-growth-faces-new-threats-1453026602.

12. http://www.cnbc.com/2017/02/27/youtube-viewers-reportedly -watch-1-billion-hours-of-videos-a-day—us-tv-viewers-watch-125 -billion-and-dropping.html.

13. "Over-the-top" services are subscription video services like Netflix, Hulu, or HBO NOW that are delivered via the Internet without requiring consumers to subscribe to a traditional cable bundle.

14. https://arstechnica.com/business/2016/07/hbo-reports-record -viewership-netflix-subscriber-additions-are-down.

15. https://techcrunch.com/2017/03/02/spotify-50-million.

16. https://www.recode.net/2017/6/5/15740956/apple-music-subscribers -new-27-million.

17. http://fortune.com/2016/08/31/cbs-all-access-ad-free.

18. http://news.wgbh.org/2016/01/26/local-news/print-dying-digital -no-savior-long-ugly-decline-newspaper-business-continues.

19. http://redef.com/original/the-truth-and-distraction-of-us-cord-cutting.

20. http://sqad.com/news/market-saturates-costs-begin-deflating-even -prime-time-not-immune.

21. http://blogs.wsj.com/cmo/2015/07/20/u-s-tv-ad-spending-fell-in -second-quarter.

22. https://www.nngroup.com/articles/banner-blindness-old-and-new -findings.

23. http://www.mediapost.com/publications/article/196071/banner -blindness-60-cant-remember-the-last-disp.html.

Chapter Two: Marketing, A Story of Deception

1. This study measures the effect of advertising on purchase preference among competitive products. In this study, a control group is shown a series of five products and asked which product they would most like to receive free. Researchers document the percentage of time each product is selected. An experimental group is then shown an advertisement for one of the products, then offered the same choice. The study examines the lift in "share of choice" for the advertised product among the experimental group, when compared with the control, demonstrating the shift

driven by the ad. In 1988, older adults who had been exposed to ads for one of the products showed a share of choice shift of 13.8 percent versus a control group that saw no ads. In the most recent study, older adults showed a share of choice of just 6.4 percent. As information flow has improved over the past decades, ad efficacy has fallen by half. The news is worse still when researchers tested millennials. Ads showed even less effect on their behavior: They shifted share of choice just 4.6 percent (http://adage.com /article/media/things-advertising-millennials/232163).

2. http://advanced-hindsight.com.

3. Dan Ariely, *Predictably Irrational: The Hidden Forces That Shape Our Decisions*, rev. ed. (New York: HarperCollins, 2009), e-book, Kindle locations 3904–13.

4. Doris Willens,*Nobody's Perfect: Bill Bernbach and the Golden Age of Advertising* (2010), e-book, Kindle locations 180–82.

5. Antonio Damasio claims pleasure and pain are "the levers the organism requires for instinctual and acquired strategies to operate efficiently." Antonio Damasio, *Descartes' Error: Emotion, Reason, and the Human Brain* (New York: Penguin Publishing Group, 2005), 262.

6. www.storynomics.com/resources/paulbloom.

7. Paul Bloom, *How Pleasure Works: The New Science of Why We Like What We Like* (New York: W. W. Norton, 2010), e-book, Kindle locations 51–52.

8. www.storynomics.com/resources/paulbloom.

9. http://www.caltech.edu/news/wine-study-shows-price-influences -perception-1374#sthash.NP9aoYLd.dpuf.

10. http://news.harvard.edu/gazette/story/2008/12/pain-is-more-intense -when-inflicted-on-purpose.

11. A promotion for ADT home security, February 23, 2016 (http://www .adt.com/?ecid=desktop-promophone-var-011816).

12. http://www.wired.com/2014/08/4-kinds-of-bad-advertising -millennials-have-killed-off.

13. http://www.emarketer.com/Article/Nearly-Two-Three-Millennials -Block-Ads/1013007.

NOTES

Chapter Three: The Evolution of Story

1. Jennifer Edson Escalas, "Narrative Processing: Building Consumer Connections to Brands," *Journal of Consumer Psychology* 14, nos. 1–2 (2004): 168–79.
2. http://humanorigins.si.edu/evidence/human-fossils.
3. https://www.scientificamerican.com/article/how-has-human-brain-evolved.
4. Antonio Damasio, *The Feeling of What Happens: Body and Emotion in the Making of Consciousness* (New York: Houghton Mifflin Harcourt, 1999).
5. John Bickle, "Empirical Evidence for a Narrative Concept of Self," in *Narrative and Consciousness: Literature, Psychology and the Brain*, ed. Gary Fireman, Ted McVay, and Owen Flanagan (New York: Oxford University Press, 2003), 195–208.
6. Sheldon Solomon, Jeff Greenberg, and Tom Pyszczynski, *The Worm at the Core: On the Role of Death in Life* (New York: Random House, 2015), 63.
7. Ernst Becker, *The Denial of Death* (New York: Free Press, 1973).
8. David M. Buss, "The New Science of Evolutionary Psychology," in *Evolutionary Psychology: The New Science of the Mind* (Boston: Pearson, 2008), 50–53.
9. N. Ramnani and A. M. Owen, "Anterior Prefrontal Cortex: Insights into Function from Anatomy and Neuroimaging," *National Review of Neuroscience* 5, no. 3 (2004): 184–94.
10. Damasio, *The Feeling of What Happens*.
11. H. C. Lau, R. D. Rogers, N. Ramnani, and R. E. Passingham, "Willed Action and Attention to the Selection of Action, *Neuroimage* 21, no. 4 (2004): 1407–15.
12. Kenneth Burke, *The Philosophy of Literary Form* (Berkeley: University of California Press, 1941).
13. Alvin I. Goldman, "Two Routes to Empathy: Insights from Cognitive Neuroscience," in *Empathy: Philosophical and Psychological Perspectives*, ed. Amy Coplan and Peter Goldie (New York: Oxford University Press, 2014).

14. Narender Ramnani and R. Christopher Miall, "A System in the Human Brain for Predicting the Actions of Others," *Nature Neuroscience* 7, no. 1 (2004), 85–90.

Chapter Five: The Full Story

1. As Simon Baron-Cohen and Paul Bloom deduce in their otherwise polemic books, *Zero Degrees of Empathy* (Baron-Cohen) and *Against Empathy* (Bloom), degrees of fellow-feeling run along a spectrum from sympathy to pity to compassion to fullhearted identification.

2. www.storynomics.com/resources/dove.

3. Daniel Kahneman and Amos Tversky (1979), "Prospect Theory: An Analysis of Decision Under Risk," *Econometrica* 47, no. 2 (1979): 263; Barry Schwartz, *The Paradox of Choice: Why More Is Less* (New York: Harper Perennial, 2004).

Chapter Six: The Purpose-Told Story

1. Jennifer Edson Escalas and Barbara B. Stern, "Sympathy and Empathy: Emotional Responses to Advertising Dramas," *Journal of Consumer Research* 29, no. 4 (March 2003): 566–78.

2. Jennifer Edson Escalas, "Imagine Yourself in the Product: Mental Simulation, Narrative Transportation, and Persuasion," *Journal of Advertising* 33, no. 2 (Summer 2004): 37–48.

3. N. Ramnani and A. M. Owen, "Anterior Prefrontal Cortex: Insights into Function from Anatomy and Neuroimaging," *National Review of Neuroscience* 5, no. 3 (2004): 184–94.

4. Charles Cooper, "If Apple Can Go Home Again, Why Not Dell?," *CNET*, May 9, 2008.

5. http://adage.com/article/news/ten-years-dove-s-real-beauty-aging/291216.

6. Melanie C. Green and Timothy C. Brock, "The Role of Transportation in the Persuasiveness of Public Narratives," *Journal of Personality and Social Psychology* 79, no. 5 (2000): 701–21.

7. Jennifer Edson Escalas, "Narrative Processing: Building Consumer Connections to Brands," *Journal of Consumer Psychology* 14, nos. 1–2 (2004): 168–79.

8. www.storynomics.com/resources/applegetamac.

9. https://www.thelocal.es/20151216/fat-chance-everything-you-need-to-know-about-spains-christmas-lottery.

10. http://time.com/4616441/el-gordo-spain-christmas-lottery-2016.

11. http://www.foxnews.com/world/2016/12/22/winners-spains-el-gordo-2-4b-lottery-take-home-418k-each.html.

Chapter Seven: Story and the CMO

1. Tom Gerace/Robert McKee interview with Linda Boff, CMO, GE, February 17, 2016, at 30 Rockefeller Plaza, New York, NY.

Chapter Eight: Storified Branding

1. Tom Gerace/Robert McKee interview with Patrick Davis, CEO, Davis Brand Capital, March 27, 2016, via Skype.

2. https://www.wsj.com/articles/epa-accuses-volkswagen-of-dodging-emissions-rules-1442595129.

3. https://www.wsj.com/articles/volkswagen-ceo-winterkorn-resigns-1443007423.

4. https://www.nytimes.com/2017/02/01/business/volkswagen-compensation-settlement-bosch-audi-porsche.html.

5. https://www.nationalgeographic.org/thisday/apr20/deepwater-horizon-explodes.

6. On Scene Coordinator Report *Deepwater Horizon* Oil Spill, submitted to the National Response Team, September 2011 (http://www.uscg.mil/foia/docs/dwh/fosc_dwh_report.pdf).

7. https://www.oilandgas360.com/bp-deepwater-horizon-lawsuit-settlement-receives-final-approval.

8. http://www.nytimes.com/2012/11/16/business/global/16iht-bp16.html.

9. http://www.telegraph.co.uk/business/2016/07/14/bp-tallies-deep-water-horizon-bill-at-almost-62bn.

10. https://www.forbes.com/sites/bertelschmitt/2017/01/30/its
    -official-volkswagen-worlds-largest-automaker-2016-or-maybe
    -toyota/#7ba0ba0276b0.

11. https://www.forbes.com/2010/07/09/worlds-biggest-oil-companies
    -business-energy-big-oil_slide_7.html.

12. 2017 Edelman Trust Barometer (www.edelman.com/trust2017).

13. One date missing from the Coca-Cola time line is 1904, when the company eliminated cocaine from its recipe. Coca-Cola's two original key ingredients were cocaine and caffeine. Cocaine was derived from the coca leaf and caffeine from kola nut, leading to the name Coca-Cola. *C* replaced the *K* in *kola* for better marketing.

14. www.storynomics.com/resources/dsm.

15. www.storynomics.com/resources/always.

16. http://news.pg.com/blog/likeagirl/SB49.

17. In 2012, UN Secretary General Ban Ki-moon launched the Sustainable Development Solutions Network (SDSN) to "mobilize global scientific and technological expertise to promote practical problem solving for sustainable development, including the design and implementation of the Sustainable Development Goals." To guide that effort, the SDSN authored and presented the first *World Happiness Report* at the UN High Level Meeting on Happiness and Well-Being that year (http://unsdsn .org/about-us/vision-and-organization).

18. J. Helliwell, R. Layard, and J. Sachs, *World Happiness Report 2017* (New York: Sustainable Development Solutions Network, 2017), 179.

Chapter Nine: Storified Advertising

1. Tom Gerace/Robert McKee interview with Linda Boff, CMO, GE, February 17, 2016, at 30 Rockefeller Plaza, New York, NY.

2. Bob Lang of TheStreet.com and RealMoney.com coined the term *FANG*, which Jim Cramer popularized, to describe Facebook, Amazon, Netflix, and Google as a group of fast-growing tech stocks in 2013. See http://www.cnbc.com/id/100436754 for details.

3. "Zazzies" is an apparent parody of Snapchat, a social application popular among the students GE is trying to reach and persuade.

4. http://punesunshine.blogspot.com/2017/04/ariel-indias-dadsshare theload-movement.html.

5. https://www.gatesnotes.com/2016-Annual-Letter.

6. https://www.nytimes.com/2015/08/24/opinion/why-arent-indias -women-working.html?_r=1.

7. http://www.creamglobal.com/case-studies/latest/17798/37377/ariel -removes-the-stains-of-social-inequality.

8. www.storynomics.com/resources/ariel.

9. http://www.creamglobal.com/case-studies/latest/17798/37377/ariel -removes-the-stains-of-social-inequality.

10. http://www.mediacom.com/en/article/index/?id=removing -the-stains-of-social-inequality.

11. https://www.bloomberg.com/news/articles/2017-05-05/fed-up -advertisers-stop-paying-more-for-declining-tv-audiences.

Chapter Ten: Storified Demand and Lead Generation

1. https://www.wsj.com/articles/average-tenure-among-chief-market ing-officers-slips-1456958118.

2. http://www.pewresearch.org/fact-tank/2014/01/09/who-is-this-man -many-americans-dont-recognize-top-news-anchor.

3. http://www.colgate.com/en/us/oc/oral-health.

4. See contentmarketingcontinuum.com to complete an evaluate your own corporation.

5. In 2014, for example, Facebook sharply reduced unpaid reach and began billing companies for this privilege. See http://adage.com/article /digital/brands-organic-facebook-reach-crashed-october/292004.

6. http://www.colgate.com/en/us/oc/oral-health.

7. A variety of techniques are employed to search engine optimize (SEO) content, including altering the text of the content, tagging content well, and adding other relevant metadata.

8. Interview with Caleb Barlow, IBM Security, March 11, 2016, Cambridge, MA.

9. *Ad Age* (http://adage.com/article/btob/ad-age-names-btob-award-winners -2016/302280) and MITX (http://www.skyword.com/contentstandard

/news/ibm-security-wins-mitx-award-for-best-b2b-marketing-website)
both honored IBM SecurityIntelligence.

10. For the sake of transparency, IBM Security is a client of co-author Tom
Gerace's company, Skyword.

11. www.storynomics.com/resources/adobe.

12. www.storynomics.com/resources/nationwide.

13. http://www.usatoday.com/story/money/2015/02/02/nationwide
-insurance-super-bowl-commercial/22734895.

14. Interview with Jeanniey Mullen, CMO, Mercer, July 10, 2017.

15. https://mercer-digital.com/insights.html.

16. http://mashable.com/2014/11/06/love-boat-princess-cruises.

17. Ibid.

18. http://www.coca-colacompany.com/our-company/coca-cola
-marketing-tops-4-billion-tripodi-says.

Chapter Eleven: Building Audience

1. http://www.nytimes.com/2015/11/03/business/media/pandora-to
-stream-serial-podcast.html.

2. World Wide Web Consortium (W3C) and the World Wide Web Foundation as of May 27, 2016 (http://www.internetlivestats.com).

3. WC3 (http://www.internetlivestats.com).

4. http://searchengineland.com/google-worlds-most-popular-search
-engine-148089.

5. https://moz.com/blog/google-organic-click-through-rates-in-2014.

6. http://www.emarketer.com/Article/Google-Will-Take-55
-of-Search-Ad-Dollars-Globally-2015/1012294.

7. Search advertising is also often called search engine marketing or SEM.

8. http://searchengineland.com/new-york-times-exposes-j-c-penney
-link-scheme-that-causes-plummeting-rankings-in-google-64529.

9. Moz blog (https://moz.com/blog/google-algorithm-cheat-sheet-panda
-penguin-hummingbird).

10. Facebook, June 21, 2013 (https://www.facebook.com/FacebookSingapore
/posts/563468333703369).

11. http://techcrunch.com/2016/01/27/facebook-earnings-q4-2015/f.

12. https://social.ogilvy.com/facebook-zero-considering-life-after-the-demise-of-organic-reach.

13. Eric Almquist and Kenneth J. Roberts, "A 'Mindshare' Manifesto" (http://membersonly.amamember.org/sales/pdf/1-Rethinking.pdf): 13.

14. https://www.forbes.com/sites/kylewong/2014/09/10/the-explosive-growth-of-influencer-marketing-and-what-it-means-for-you/#1edd522552ac.

15. https://www.nytimes.com/2016/08/30/business/media/instagram-ads-marketing-kardashian.html?_r=0.

16. http://www.marketwatch.com/story/do-celebrity-endorsements-work-1300481444531.

17. Kendall Jenner was reportedly paid $250,000 to tweet about the Fyre Festival (https://news.vice.com/story/fyre-fest-organizers-blew-all-their-money-months-early-on-models-planes-and-yachts). The festival failed to deliver the luxury accommodations, food, or entertainment promised, leaving travelers stranded (https://www.nytimes.com/2017/04/28/arts/music/fyre-festival-ja-rule-bahamas.html).

18. WOMMA, "Return on Word of Mouth," November 2013 (https://womma.org/wp-content/uploads/2015/09/STUDY-WOMMA-Return-on-WOM-Executive-Summary.pdf).

19. www.storynomics.com/resources/mastercard.

20. Robert McKee/Tom Gerace interview with Raja Rajamannar, February 2, 2016, at Mastercard Headquarters, Purchase, NY.

21. http://www.janrain.com/about/newsroom/press-releases/online-consumers-fed-up-with-irrelevant-content-on-favorite-websites-according-to-janrain-study.

22. Neolane and the Direct Marketing Association, "Realtime Marketing Insights Study," July 2013 (https://blogs.adobe.com/digitalmarketing/social-media/highlights-realtime-marketing-insights-study).

23. Skyword Inc. personalization performance results across multiple brands, February 2017.

24. http://traveler.marriott.com.

25. TrueView is a pre-roll advertising product available from Google's YouTube.

26. Robert McKee/Tom Gerace interview with David Beebe, December 16, 2016.

Chapter Twelve: Storified Sales

1. Sales Performance Optimization Surveys 2011–2015, CSOInsights.com, a subsidiary of MHI Global.

2. Sales Performance Optimization 2015 Survey, CSOInsights.com, a subsidiary of MHI Global.

3. https://www.usfhealthonline.com/resources/healthcare/electronic-medical-records-mandate.

4. https://www.cbo.gov/sites/default/files/recurringdata/51298-2017-01-healthinsurance.pdf.

Chapter Thirteen: -Nomics

1. https://www.semrush.com/info/colgate.com+(by+organic).

2. Disclosure: One of the authors of this book, Tom Gerace, is founder and CEO of Skyword.

Conclusion

1. http://www.independent.co.uk/arts-entertainment/tv/news/game-of-thrones-season-6-hbo-spends-over-10m-on-each-episode-a6959651.html.

2. http://www.cinemablend.com/television/Insane-Amount-Money-Netflix-Spend-Content-2016-112117.html.

3. http://adage.com/article/cmo-strategy/pg-hiking-ad-spend/303731.

4. https://www.theguardian.com/technology/2015/jan/29/virtual-reality-documentary-middle-man-journalism-chris-milk-film.

5. www.storynomics.com/resources/ariel.

INDEX